THE
WHITE HOUSE PRESS
ON THE PRESIDENCY

News Management and Co-option

Frank Cormier
James Deakin
Helen Thomas

Edited by
Kenneth W. Thompson

UNIVERSITY
PRESS OF
AMERICA

LANHAM • NEW YORK • LONDON

THE WHITE HOUSE PRESS ON THE PRESIDENCY:

NEWS MANAGEMENT AND CO-OPTION

VOLUME IV IN A SERIES
FUNDED BY THE
JOHN and MARY R. MARKLE FOUNDATION

Copyright © 1983 by

University Press of America,™ Inc.

4720 Boston Way
Lanham, MD 20706

3 Henrietta Street
London WC2E 8LU England

Library of Congress Cataloging in Publication Data

Main entry under title:

The White House Press on the presidency.

Contents: Preface/Kenneth W. Thompson—Intro-
duction/Kenneth W. Thompson—The problem of
presidential-press relations/James Deakin—[etc.]
   1.Presidents—United States—Press conferences—
Addresses, essays, lectures. 2. Reagan, Ronald—
Views on the press—Addresses, essays, lectures.
3. Government and the press—United States—Addresses,
essays, lectures. I. Thompson, Kenneth W., 1921-
II. Cormier, Frank. Co-option of the press. 1983.
III. Deakin, James, 1929-   . The problem of
presidential press relations. 1983. IV. Thomas, Helen,
1920-   . Ronald Reagan and the management of the
news. 1983.
E839.5.W49   1983   353.03'5   83-6708
ISBN 0-8191-3254-3
ISBN 0-8191-3255-1 (pbk.)

THE WHITE HOUSE PRESS ON THE PRESIDENCY:

NEWS MANAGEMENT AND CO-OPTION

*Dedicated
to*

*all those who seek a better
understanding
of presidential-press relations*

TABLE OF CONTENTS

PREFACE

In the autumn of 1980, the Miller Center of Public Affairs published a widely discussed report on presidential press conferences which carried the imprimatur of a distinguished national commission co-chaired by Governor Linwood Holton and Ray Scherer. In the winter of 1981, James Brady in introducing President Reagan's first press conference announced that the Reagan administration would follow the recommendations of the Miller Center commission. These included a requirement that reporters wishing to ask questions raise their hands and be recognized by the President so that the circus atmosphere of the questioning might be replaced by some reasonable measure of decorum. The commission also called for greater regularity in the holding of press conferences, a practice which has not been fully observed by the Reagan administration any more than it was by its immediate predecessors.

In preparation for the report, the staff of the Miller Center consulted widely with some of America's most respected journalists and reporters while at the same time interviewing some of the best known press secretaries in recent administrations. The present volume draws together the opinions of three senior White House reporters who together have probably covered more presidents than any similar group of reporters. Two of them will be recognized as reporters who have opened and closed the press conferences of recent American presidents. Under President Reagan, Helen Thomas continues the tradition of Frank Cormier and Merriman Smith with past administrations of bringing the Reagan press conferences to a close with the famous phrase "Thank you, Mr. President."

The three reporters whose views are laid bare in this discussion were born in Missouri, Kentucky and Massachusetts and have come into prominence from differing educational and news backgrounds. What they share in common is a conviction that White House reporters must pursue the truth wherever it may lead them. They are

1

united in opposition to what they consider news management or co-option of reporters by particular presidents, although at least two of them acknowledge that on more than one occasion they have been subject to the beguiling approaches of a particular president.

As a group, they are impatient with the view that certain issues may be so sensitive that full press coverage at a certain stage, say, of delicate international negotiations should be shielded from public disclosure (one of them would accept no restraints while the other two take a more qualified position). They are critical of the typical press briefing by the press officer and resent being herded together for what they contemptuously refer to as press or "photo opportunities." They single out Franklin D. Roosevelt and John F. Kennedy as model presidents in their relations with the press although the latter does not escape criticism.

It becomes crystal clear from their accounts that the atmosphere of press conferences has undergone a revolutionary change in the television era. The Roosevelt press conferences with a score of reporters gathered in the Oval Room has been replaced by kleig lights and hundreds of newsmen some of whom have only marginal knowledge of presidential politics. A graduate student whose father has contributed to a presidential campaign is accredited alongside the so-called Washington regulars. The gains for democracy must be balanced with the tendency of the Walter Lippmanns or James Restons of the day to absent themselves from most press conferences. Recent presidents have come to see press conferences as ordeals more than opportunities.

Nonetheless, leading White House reporters continue to view presidential press conferences, if not as the equivalent of the British "question period" in the Parliament, as forums for gaining clarification on national policies and for testing the president as a leader. Rather than allowing doubts and concerns to pile up, they maintain that an ongoing dialogue between the president and the self-acknowledged interrogators for the public can serve the national interest. Responsible journalists consider themselves the surrogates of the public asking the questions the public would ask if present at a press conference.

Certain passages in this little volume echo with convictions about the first amendment, the public's right to know and freedom of the press. The angle of vision is of course that of experienced White House reporters. Their opinions are those of a particular profession skilled in ferreting out a story. The missing chair in the debate is that of press secretaries and political leaders and the Miller Center is determined to publish a companion volume in which such voices are heard. To paraphrase Clemenceau, the subject is too important to be left exclusively to reporters.

Having said that, we believe that the papers and the discussion published herewith may help to illuminate some of the most important questions on the presidency and the press. Students and citizens must form their own judgments on matters of utmost importance to a free people.

We thank the John and Mary Markle Foundation for the financial support which made this volume possible. I am indebted to my colleagues Blaire French, Shirley Kingsbury and Clyde Lutz who helped in countless ways in the preparation of this manuscript.

INTRODUCTION

I'd like to welcome all of you to the Miller Center in our ongoing examination of the relationship between the president and the press. Although we've held several colloquia of various types to discuss this subject, we've felt that there was a dimension of this problem we hadn't really tapped. We've talked about high principles and general theories—and the three of you are certainly interested in that—but neglected the day-to-day relationship, what somebody called the nuts and bolts of presidential-press relations, including the question of news management and the issue of presidents seeking to co-opt the press. We've really not dealt with some of these things, in any systematic way. And as we talked with each of you preparatory to this meeting, it appeared that this was something that might be worth doing. So we thought we would begin with some reflections and comments by Jim Deakin. Then we'll go on to Helen and Frank.

Jim Deakin needs no introduction to this group. All of you know him. He's either left an honest life to engage in the kind of thing that most people around this table do all the time, being a teacher and a scholar, or he's moved from a less honest to an honest life, depending on your point of view. He began as a reporter and local staff member for the *St. Louis Post-Dispatch* from 1951 to 1953. He was White House correspondent for the *Post-Dispatch* from 1955 to 1980, covering Presidents Eisenhower through Carter. He was a member of the Washington bureau of the *Post-Dispatch* from 1953 to 1980. He has engaged in extensive travel covering summit conferences, two trips to Russia with President Nixon, all presidential campaigns from 1956 through 1976. He has covered the Congress, federal regulatory agencies and written on economic policies. His honest or dishonest life newly arrived at is as Adjunct Associate Professor of Journalism and Faculty Associate of George Washington University. He was before that a fellow of the Woodrow Wilson International Center for Scholars. He is the author of *The Lobbyists,* which deals with lobbyists and lobbying techniques. He is also the author of *Lyndon Johnson's Credibility Gap,* co-author of *Smiling Through the Apocalypse,* co-author of *The Presidency and the Press* and is currently engaged in writing a book on the news media and the government. He has written for *Esquire,* the *New Republic,* the *New York Times* and for many other publications. He has made television and radio appearances on Face the Nation, Washington Week in Review, Panorama, the Bill Moyers show, BBC, Canadian Broadcasting Corporation and others. He has received a distinguished alumnus citation from Washington University, and was president of the White House Correspondents Association from 1974 to 1975. He was awarded the Merriman Smith award for White House reporting in 1977 and received a research grant from the Markle Foundation in 1981. He was born in St. Louis and educated at John Burroughs school in St. Louis and Washington University. His current residence is in Bethesda, Maryland. We're very grateful to Jim not only for agreeing to make our opening presentation this morning but also for speaking later in the afternoon on *The Imperial President and the Imperial Media.* This morning he is going to open our discussion with some reflections and analyses of press secretaries.

THE PROBLEM OF PRESIDENTIAL–PRESS RELATIONS

James Deakin

MR. DEAKIN: Thank you, Ken. Between George Washington and Jimmy Carter, thirty-eight men served as President of the United States. Each conducted the office according to his ability, his intellect, his personality, his temperament, predispositions, his educational, cultural, family and economic background, the circumstances under which he became president, his political skills, the events that took place during his presidency and the economic conditions and social values of his time, the state of human knowledge at that moment and the inability of humankind to predict the future. And each of these presidents had trouble with the press. Why?

The relationship between the president and the press is the Jarndyce versus Jarndyce of relationships—an endless dispute. There is no single comprehensive explanation for the chronic stresses and strains between the government and the press. Instead, there is an interminable list of reasons. The government desires to conduct much of its business secretly. The press desires to penetrate that secrecy. The government has great difficulty in obtaining enough information to enable it to make wise decisions. Operating with inadequate information in the first place, the government then frustrates and angers the press by giving it only part of that. The government wishes to withhold public comment or specific action until it gets more information. The press impatiently demands immediate comment or specific action. The government wishes to remain silent while it is reaching its decisions. The press wishes to report the decisionmaking process while it is going on. The government wishes to manipulate the

7

press. It spends at least a billion dollars annually and employs an estimated 19,000 publicity agents in a tireless effort to use thè news media advantageously. The press does not wish to be exploited by the government; however, its vigilance is not eternal. The government seeks maximum publicity for most although not all of its policies once they have been formulated. The press insists on picking and choosing what it will emphasize or neglect. The government wants most although not all of its actions adequately reported and explained. The press frustrates and angers the government by reporting and explaining inaccurately, incompletely or prejudicially. Occasionally it manages to do all three in the same story. The government wishes its point of view to prevail. It believes its policies are the correct courses of action for the nation. The press reports the government's position. Then it insists on reporting other points of view. The government, except on rare, heartening occasions, does not wish to have its mistakes brought to public attention. The press brings the government's mistakes to public attention. The government, composed as it is of human beings, does not like to be criticized. The press criticizes the government. The government and the press then disagree over whether a mistake was actually a mistake. They disagree over whether criticism was justified. They disagree.

The causes of conflict are endless. There is no satisfactory way to summarize them. But one phrase comes close: Conflicting purposes. The government and the press simply have conflicting purposes. The purposes are not only different, they actually conflict. And because their purposes are so dissimilar, their perceptions differ. The government and the press see things in very different ways. None of these problems can be solved. None of the conflicts can be removed. The fundamental differences between the government and the press are beyond the wit of man to reconcile. But that is not a bad thing. It is a good thing. The differences should not be reconciled. The government should continue on its course and the press on its course, as imperfect and unsatisfactory as these courses often are. Unquestionably there can and should be improvements. The government could be less secretive and manipulative if it chose to be. This would benefit the nation, not harm it. The news media could be less superficial, less hasty and less sensational if they chose to be. This certainly would benefit the nation, as the nation is superficial enough already. But the basic conflicts should not be removed. The government and the press should function at arms length. When they do not stay apart, when their purposes are forced into an artificial and unnatural agreement, the nation *is* harmed. The Bay of Pigs episode was an object lesson in what happens when the purposes of the government and the purposes of the press are made to coincide.

When it is realized that the basic conflicts are irreconcilable there are two possible outcomes. There can be an accommodation, a modus vivendi based on at least a modicum of understanding. John and Mary Bickerson settled down for a lifetime of acrimony, suspicion and uneasy tolerance. They cannot abide each other but each comprehends that the other has a place in the grand democratic experiment. The Republican editor William Allen White wrote of Franklin Roosevelt, "We who hate your gaudy guts salute you." That was an accommodation. Or there can be a siege. When the siege mentality takes over at the White House all communications ceases. Not even a scant understanding is possible. The president and his subordinates come to believe that remorseless forces of the media are implacably bent on their destruction. The White House is a beleaguered entrenchment and the enemy is the press. A list of enemies is drawn up with vengeance sworn. And the paranoia spreads outward until the president and his people are convinced that not just the press but almost everyone is out to get them. Walter Cronkite has come out against the war. The Supreme Court has struck us a fell blow with a tape recorder. Bob Hope is for gun control. All is indubitably lost. The siege mentalities of Lyndon Johnson and Richard Nixon radically altered the relationship between the government and the news media. But the matter went much deeper than that. The animosity between these two presidents and the reporters who covered them was only a symptom. If it had been only a press/government squabble the nation would have sailed right along relatively unconcerned. Bickering between presidents and journalists was nothing new. However, the American people were not left out of it. They were not merely spectators at an entertaining little spectacle in the journalistic coliseum. Lions one, Christians zero, Bill Moyers used to say. Johnson and Nixon grossly distorted the relationship between the people and the government, not just between the press and government. In their ten and a half years in office these two presidents shattered the confidence of the American people and changed political attitudes almost beyond recognition. There had been cynicism before; now cynicism became epidemic. There had been uncertainty before; now uncertainty became chronic.

Not all of this anxiety can be laid at the door of two presidents. The nuclear specter so profoundly affected humanity's outlook that the overriding political question of the late Twentieth Century became species survival. These were the years, moreover, when Americans first confronted the full meaning of environmental despoliation, intractable inflation, the transfer of national wealth to a foreign cartel, and a host of other miseries. Historians began comparing the Twentieth Century to the Dark Ages. Authors grew rich on books forecasting the ultimate smash-up. Americans had once spoken confidently of their manifest destiny. Now they contemplated their manifest danger. The American Century, a conceit of Henry Luce and other deep offenders, lasted 30 years. Easy come, easy go.

But the point insofar as Johnson and Nixon were concerned was that the more horrors there were, the more fortitude they required. The American people had to find more courage. Otherwise in their new vulnerability they ran a strong risk of succumbing to the politics of fear and hate. Johnson and Nixon took away the fortitude. The American people had not been so naive as to suppose that their government never lied. But they were not prepared for lying as a consistent official policy. Johnson gave them that. They had understood that rogues occasionally achieved high office. But they were unaccustomed to criminals who plotted crimes in the White House. Nixon gave them that. The followers could no longer have confidence in the leader. The government could not help the people face the dangers. They had to go it alone. Some bought shelters and stocked them with weapons. Others went in for manic moralities. The change in political attitudes as a result of Johnson and Nixon was so great that their predecessors seem almost as remote as Main Street. The immediate post-war presidents, Truman, Eisenhower and Kennedy, are part of an idyllic past. Gone where the woodbine twineth. Vanished on the soft summer air. Of course those post-war years were not idyllic at all. But compared with the situation under Johnson and Nixon the attitude of the people toward their leaders was normal: frequently critical, exasperated or indignant but not abnormal. That was the difference. That is what is really meant when it is said that Vietnam and Watergate transformed the relationship between the press and the government. It actually means they transformed the relationship between the *people* and the government. Presidents, journalists and citizens struggle to cope with the present while trying to snatch a few moments to come to terms with the past. In the nature of things they are given very little time for reflection. Politics is not Proustian. Events proceed. New problems arise. The Presidents who came after Johnson and Nixon—Gerald R. Ford and Jimmy Carter—did not notably restore the presidency as a source of fortitude. So in large measure the Johnson-Nixon distortion remains, still affecting the news media, still affecting the nation.

Now, each president deals with the press in his own way. The machinery is essentially the same in every administration, and so are the techniques. Each president uses the standard equipment, but each uses it according to the dictates of his personality. On the mechanical level, for instance, no modern president would think of operating without a press secretary. Richard Nixon was the only contemporary president who considered doing away with this familiar piece of machinery. Desiring to demonstrate his disdain for journalists, Nixon decided not to have a press secretary. Nixon never could feel good about anything, but this gave him a certain satisfaction. However, it turned out to be impractical. He soon found it necessary to elevate Ronald Ziegler from the lowly status of press assistant to the loftier title of press secretary. All blessings are mixed.

So every president has a press secretary. But that is only a serviceable generalization. There is a great deal of latitude. There are many variations and nuances. Eisenhower held press conferences regularly. He was very dutiful about it. Other than that, however, he left relations with the news media in the hands of his press secretary. He did this because he had great faith in Jim Hagerty and because it saved a lot of work. That was important. Kennedy was basically his own press secretary. This was partly because he liked reporters and was not afraid of them, but mostly it was simply because he wanted to handle his own press relations. He believed he could do it better than anyone else, and this self-confidence communicated itself to the press. It was half the battle.

Johnson tried it both ways and succeeded at neither. Sometimes he was his own press secretary and sometimes he left it to An Unfortunate. He tried everything. He tried being as friendly as all get-out. Then he tried being aloof, like Charles de Gaulle, but, funny, he no look like de Gaulle. He tried blandishment: "You stick with me," he would tell a reporter, "and I'll make you a big man." He appealed to the better angels of journalism's nature: "I know you don't like your cornpone president." Or to the ultimate pragmatism: "Remember, I am the only president you've got." Nothing worked. Johnson thought there was some secret to it. If he just tried harder, he could solve the mystery and make those smart, mean, ungrateful news bastards like him and do what he wanted them to do. He was convinced that Kennedy had known the secret and many other secrets of charisma while he, Lyndon Johnson, did not. For which he admired and hated Kennedy. Johnson could not live with what he had.

Nixon left press relations to his press secretary once he had reconciled himself to having one. But this was not a matter of faith in the expertise of Ronald Ziegler. Nixon was nutty but not stupid. It was simply because he loathed and feared reporters. Absolutely despised them. Wished to avoid contact with them. On presidential trips most of the press travels on a separate plane but a small pool of reporters accompanies the president on Air Force One. The pool is confined to a small area in the rear of the plane. Nixon liked to say, "It smells bad back there." Once he came into the rear area when the reporters were not there. Pointing to the empty press seats, he commented to a group of Air Force stewards and Secret Service agents: "It sure smells better back here, doesn't it?" The word got around.

Ford and Carter were more traditional in their press relations. They held press conferences, not with the frequency of Franklin Roosevelt, twice a week without fail for twelve years except during the war, but often enough to breathe a little life into an institution that had almost died under Nixon. Neither Ford nor Carter left press relations entirely to their press secretaries as Ike did. But neither did they try to emulate Kennedy and be their own press secretaries. They fell somewhere in-between. Ford did not dislike or fear reporters. It was not in him to dislike very many people deeply. He was not quick at discerning motives or meanings. This meant he could be victimized. The reporters liked Jerry Ford. It was impossible not to. But on the other hand they had known him a long time. They were patient with him. The general belief was that Nixon had chosen him for vice president as a precaution. Congress would never impeach Nixon if it meant Ford would be President. A trick a day.

Carter's attitude towards reporters was complicated. Certainly he distrusted them, that is par for the course, and he may have disliked them intensely. But his real feelings about reporters, I suspect, was the same as his basic attitude toward everyone in his political life: moral superiority. Those who agreed with him were enlightened and virtuous. Those who disagreed with him or criticized him were benighted. Forsaken by God, prohibited from heaven, and just plain wrong. Carter was a barefoot Calvin. He was also a whiner. That was not so good for fortitude.

Statistics are not a reliable guide to the role of a presidential press secretary. Eisenhower was in office eight years and had only one press secretary, Hagerty. Nixon was in office five and a half years and had one press secretary, Ziegler. Carter was in office four years and had one press secretary, Jody Powell. But while Hagerty and Powell had substantial power and influence, Ziegler had very little. This, as it turned out, saved his skin. However, the fact that Hagerty and Powell had a lot of clout did not mean that they were similar in other respects. Hagerty knew a great deal about journalism. Powell knew very little.

Kennedy was president for not quite three years and had one press secretary, Pierre Salinger. Johnson was pesident for five years and had five press secretaries—Pierre Salinger, George Reedy, Bill Moyers, Robert Fleming, and George Christian—six if Joe Laitin is counted, and he should be. Things were never simple with Johnson. Once he had two press secretaries at the same time. Ford served two and a half years and had two press secretaries, but one of them was done in by his principles. After only a month on the job, Gerald terHorst resigned when Ford pardoned Nixon. TerHorst was succeeded by Ron Nessen who told reporters he was a Ron but not a Ziegler. Peter Lisagor of the *Chicago Daily News* immediately commented that two Rons don't make a right. Lisagor apparently knew something.

Some press secretaries have been good at the technical side of their job. Others have been policymakers or at least candidate members of the Presidium. Others have not been notably proficient in either role. Hagerty, by all measurements the best press secretary in history, was a superb technician, but he also dominated the Eisenhower administration's press policy and operated in some other policy areas as well. Salinger understood the technical journalistic aspects of the job but was not greatly interested in them. He had a voice in press policy, but on other important issues he was not in Kennedy's innermost circle of advisors. Kennedy was informed on October 15, 1962 that aerial photographs had revealed Soviet missiles in Cuba. But Salinger was not told about them until October 21, seven days later. Salinger was an intelligent, witty, somewhat cynical man. He conducted day-to-day press relations with a sort of sloppy verve, but on the whole, capably. On the big stuff, however, he was strictly an adjunct to Kennedy.

Lyndon Johnson so arranged things that it was difficult for any member of his staff to do a good job. After Kennedy was assassinated, Salinger stayed on for a while at LBJ's urging. Then he departed for California to pursue a political career, and Reedy became press secretary. One day Johnson told a group of reporters, including myself, that Salinger had called him from California about a problem facing the administration. Johnson said Salinger had an idea for coping with the problem. The President was impressed. "An honest-to-God idea," said LBJ. "That's the kind of people Kennedy had; they had ideas." Then, his voice dripping with scorn, he said, "And who have I got? *George Reedy.*" When, later on, George Christian became press secretary, Johnson warned him to be wary in dealing with the White House reporters. "Remember," he said, "these people are smarter than you are." He was an absolute wonder at building morale.

Struggling along under these ringing endorsements, Johnson's press secretaries did the best they could. When Reedy was left alone to do his job, which wasn't often, he could be impressive. His briefing on a national railroad strike was a memorable performance. Thoroughly conversant with the subject, Reedy guided the reporters patiently and skillfully through the issues and complexities of the strike. It was his finest hour, but there weren't many of them as most of Reedy's weary days were spent being one of Johnson's punching bags. Moyers, who succeeded Reedy, had little interest in the technical side of the job: announcements, briefings, arranging coverage of events, travel schedules and the like. He preferred the role of policymaker. What Moyers liked to do was to sit down with one or two reporters in his office and talk about the President's options and alternatives in a given situation. Some reporters did not trust Moyers. They believed he misled them. In my conversations with Moyers I never got the impression he was deceiving me, at least not outrageously. And even if he was, it paled by comparison with the old master.

Robert Fleming, then chief of ABC's Washington bureau, had an interesting experience. One day in 1966, Johnson persuaded him to join the White House staff. At a press conference, Johnson announced that Fleming would have the title of deputy press secretary but actually would be "my press secretary." The president emphasized this. He said Fleming "will be doing a good deal of the press secretary's work. As far as I am concerned I will want to call him my press secretary." It seemed that Fleming would be the press secretary.

Things are not 'what they seem. In a few masterly words, doublespeak destroyed Bob Fleming. A reporter asked whether Moyers would still have the title of press secretary. Johnson replied, "Special assistant to the President, it has always been that. You can call him press secretary, though, if it gives you any thrill . . . I don't object to what you call him." Johnson told the reporters they could go right on getting information from Moyers: "If you can't get to me, you can get to Bill. If you can't get to him, you can get to Fleming. I have no objection to your getting to anyone you want to if they know what I am thinking." But Fleming would be "my press secretary." Now we are two.

The reporters considered the situation. They knew Johnson and

Moyers were very close, almost a tyrant-and-son relationship. They figured Fleming would have a tough time developing that kind of relationship; hell, he would have a tough time developing any relationship short of evisceration. They knew Moyers was familiar with top-level policy matters, was willing to talk about them and was articulate, although they were never sure whether he was talking about Johnson's policy or Moyers' policy. Johnson, who had the soul of a KGB agent, knew all about the little sessions in Moyers' office. He was saying in effect that they could continue. They did. After a while, Fleming just faded away. It is cold in Washington.

The last ones in from the cold were George Christian, a technician, and Joseph Laitin, a survivor. Christian was phlegmatically competent and competently phlegmatic. He was Lyndon Johnson's last press secretary and he held the job for two years—an achievement. Laitin never had the title of press secretary. The highest he got was "acting." He was a press spokesman and friend to mankind in several administrations.

With Ron Ziegler and Ron Nessen, the modern press secretaryship hit rock bottom. Ziegler was the creature of Harry Robbins (Bob) Haldeman, a California advertising man who prepared for national destiny by hustling Sani-flush and Black Flag bug killer. An endless supply of Ron Zieglers is available in Washington. They are the White House's cannon fodder. Generation after generation of blank young men stamped monotonously from the great American machine, with eager dentition and Orphan Annie eyes that reflect no light. They were born not yesterday but this morning. On one occasion, Ziegler was asked to comment on an action by the Group of Ten, the name given to the leading industrial nations. An internal struggle took place up there on the press secretary's podium. It was obvious Ziegler had never heard of the Group of Ten. However, he wished to contrive an answer that would not reveal his ignorance. You could almost see the wheels turn. "Well," Ziegler said finally, "we're not committed to any particular number."

Ron Nessen, a former television reporter, illustrated an important phenomenon. A president's staff tends to find a certain level and the level it finds is the president's level. Nessen was fully up to the standard of Jerry Ford.

Jimmy Carter's press secretary, Jody Powell, illustrated another point. Although Nessen's example made it clear that journalistic experience does not guarantee a successful press secretary, experience is better than nothing. Powell was intelligent and quick-witted, but he had never been a reporter or editor. He picked up some things as he went along, but he never had the kind of journalistic "feel" that Hagerty, Salinger and Reedy had. Journalism is an experiential, sensory occupation. Powell knew the theory but not the practice. Without any intimate career understanding of the reporters who confronted him each day in the briefing room, he had nothing with which to balance his fierce loyalty to Carter. There was no leavening, only a flat one-sided advocacy of the president. Powell cracked a lot of jokes, and they carried him for a while but it soon became apparent that he was only a Carter partisan. No shadings. One day during the transition from Ford to Carter, Nessen briefed the press as usual and then conferred with Powell to discuss the changeover. He asked Powell whether he wanted to meet with the reporters. "No," said Powell, "they've had their feeding for today." This exhange was overheard. The animals thus knew where they stood. The relationship was to be only "we-and-they." It was not to be "we-and-they-but-they-have-a-point-too."

Some political scientists conceive that the press secretary serves two masters. They commiserate with him in his schizophrenia. But he does not serve two masters. He serves the president. The reporters expect the press secretary to be a partisan. They do not expect him to be an advocate of their objectives. The sun has not yet risen in the west. But a press secretary who has some journalistic background can, if he chooses, communicate the feel and taste of journalism to the president and the White House staff. He may venture to educate them from time to time in the mysterious ways and repugnant purposes of the news media. Acknowledging that these are detestable, he nevertheless conveys the idea that they are there and will not go away. This must be done delicately. The reporters know immediately, God knows how they know but they do, when they have a press secretary who occasionally undertakes some two-way communication between the president and the press room. It is very rare. But when it happens, the relationship between the reporters and the press secretary is subtly affected. He is still a partisan, but there are some shadings. The reporters know that he belongs heart and gizzard to the president, but they suspect that somewhere down deep is the primeval memory of a city editor.

The question is: does the president listen? If his press secretary tries to interpret the press to him, does he pay attention? The press secretary can summon spirits from the vasty deep, but will they come? And why should the president listen? What difference will it make? If the press secretary has a rapport with those fickle characters in the press room, does that really help the president? They will turn on him

at the first hint of trouble or weakness. And how they will. What good
will goodwill do then?

The answers are in the problems, those large, adamantine problems
that cannot be solved but can be accommodated. And especially the
problem of the siege mentality. It may help avoid the siege mentality.
Hagerty did this for Eisenhower. Salinger didn't need to do it for
Kennedy. Johnson was unteachable. Nixon was unreachable.
Nessen, if he recognized the opportunity, passed it up. And Powell
either didn't know or wasn't interested.

Some Presidents are reasonably secure in themselves or in the
affection of the voters. As a result, their dealings with the news media,
although highly important, do not become an overriding or neurotic
preoccupation. These presidents grumble and complain about the
press. It is a constant irritant to them, but they accept its place in life's
miscellany. They agree to a modus vivendi with the media, a
temporary and precarious live-and-let-live that enables the work to go
forward. In modern times, Eisenhower, Kennedy and Ford were in
this category; in the past, Jefferson (the foremost dichotomist of
antiquity, the original "love-the-press-hate-the-press" president), the
two Roosevelts and above all Lincoln. A cosmic sense of humor helps:

Lincoln: "Reporter of the (New York) *Herald,* eh? Well, I'm not
afraid of you. Walk right in and sit right down."

Reporter: "Mr. President, I was sent up here by the editor of the
Herald to ascertain, if possible, the motive of your sudden visit to this
place. [Lincoln was inspecting a gun factory.] Perhaps you will
consider it impertinent for me to enquire into such a subject."

Lincoln: "No, sir, I do not consider it in any way an impertinence.
At worst it might be thought an imprudence. . . You gentlemen of the
press seem to be pretty much like soldiers, who have to go wherever
sent, whatever may be the dangers or difficulties in the way. God
forbid I should by any rudeness of speech or manner make your duties
any harder than they are . . . If I am not afraid of you, it is because I feel
you are trustworthy. That is to say, I have no fear you will violate
confidences or make improper use of any words I may let fall.

"The press has no better friend than I am—no one who is more
ready to acknowledge its great power—its tremendous power for both
good and evil. I would like it always on my side, if it could be so; so
much, so very much depends upon sound public ópinion. Mr. Bennett
is an extraordinary exponent of that truth; he can do what he likes with
the public in many ways. He is a great editor, and his paper is a great
paper—the greatest in this country, perhaps, if my good friend Horace
Greeley will allow me to say so . . .

"Ah, do you gentlemen who control so largely public opinion, do you ever think how much you might lighten the burdens of men in power—those poor unfortunates weighed down by care, anxieties and responsibilities? If you would only give them a consistent and hearty support, bearing patiently with them when they seem to be making mistakes and giving them credit at least for good intentions, when these seem not to be clear, what comfort you would bestow!"

(The reporter assures Lincoln that nothing objectionable would be printed.)

Lincoln: "I trust you sir, I trust you . . . My allusion had no present application. As to your question concerning my motive in coming here, you may say to your editor it has not been caused by any crisis in the affairs of the nation."

Well. Peel the layers off of that one. Flattery, sympathy, charm, sarcasm, cleverness, wariness, pathos, beguilement, seduction—down, down, down into the depths of Lincoln. And at the bottom he is laughing. He is laughing at the reporter, at the egregious editor of the *Herald,* James Gordon Bennet, who was known to his contemporaries as "the Prince of Darkness," and he is laughing at himself as he observes his own performance. Why did Lincoln laugh? If that could be answered we would know unknowable things. But no matter . . .

Incidentally, he never told the reporter why he was visiting the gun factory.

Lincoln was a public relations artist. Although he liked to say that his policy was to have no policy, it was evident that his policy was to preserve the Union by doing three things: Hold the borderstates, especially Kentucky; find generals who would fight, and keep public opinion with him. He was tireless in wooing and flattering the most influential editors of the day: Bennett of the *Herald,* Henry Raymond of the *New York Times* and Horace Greeley of the *New York Tribune.* More important, he concentrated on addressing the nation as a whole, not the Washington press corps. This technique was much favored by some later presidents. Richard Nixon set up an entire White House apparatus to bypass the Washington reporters and appeal directly to the public. Everyone needs a role model.

Lincoln's accute public relations instinct did not make him unique among presidents. Nor did it insulate him from criticism. God knows it didn't. What set Lincoln apart from most presidents was his sense of humor in dealing with the press—he said he didn't *read* newspapers, he *skirmished* with them. Among modern presidents, only Franklin

Roosevelt and John F. Kennedy ever found anything to laugh about when it came to the news media.

At a press conference on May 9, 1962, Kennedy was asked how he felt about press coverage of his administration. The first part of his reply, that he was reading more and enjoying it less, has endured as a political epigram. But the rest of the reply was more significant. It epitomized the rare president who is secure enough within himself to *accept* the news media:

> Well, I am reading more and enjoying it less, and so on, but I have not complained nor do I plan to make any general complaints. I read and talk to myself about it but I don't plan to issue any general statement on the press. I think that they are doing their task, as a critical branch, the Fourth estate. I am attempting to do mine. And we are going to live together for a period, and then go our separate ways.

That was a *modus vivendi.*

It is not clear where Lincoln got his inner security. Kennedy presumably derived his from the fact that he grew up surrounded by a half billion dollars. There is absolutely nothing like a half billion dollars for inner security. Most presidents are not this fortunate in their formative years. And the least fortunate of all are those who spent their childhood with their noses pressed against the window of the candy store. We should not elect presidents who were never once allowed *inside* the candy store. Unless we are so insightful as to discern a Lincoln. That is the trick.

"With exceptions so rare that they are regarded as miracles and freaks of nature, successful democratic politicians are insecure men," wrote Walter Lippmann. For some politicians, the rise to the top is a grim affair. These are the driven men. Their psychological landscape is bleak, their emotional existence precarious. Politics—or life itself, for that matter—is in no sense pleasurable. It is a relentless struggle against tormentors, opponents and betrayers. For these men, ambition is the mask of their insecurity, cynicism the consequence. They must, Lippmann wrote, "placate, appease, bribe, seduce, bamboozle or otherwise manipulate" the electorate. They must overcome, by force or guile, the many strong egos that are ranged against them as they battle toward the prize. Every man's hand is against them. And none more so than the press.

The press is the enemy. It is eternally to be guarded against. It is never to be accepted as part of a multi-hued democratic tapestry. There can be no temporary *modus vivendi*. These politicians pay lip service to the theory of a free press, just as they can make obeisance to any theory, any opinion, any interest that is necessary to their success. To them Paris is always worth a mass. But they do not believe the press should be free. Not really. Not down where they live.

MR. THOMPSON: Any comments or questions?

MR. CORMIER: Well, there was one thing that struck me. You suggested that something immutable happened with Johnson and Nixon in the relationship between the public and the president.

MR. DEAKIN: Not immutable. Simply that they are still affected by it.

MR. CORMIER: I wonder if we are that much. I'm thinking not of the press but of the electorate. It seems to me that the electorate shows a great capacity to go along with Ronald Reagan, for instance. They want to believe. The public wants to believe.

MR. DEAKIN: Would we have a movement for a nuclear freeze in this country if the people trusted their government?

MR. CORMIER: No. I guess you're right on that.

MR. DEAKIN: The cynicism, the distrust of government has always been there. All people distrust their central government. You will find no people in the world more distrustful than the French peasants living a great distance from Paris. They do not trust the government, they never have in their entire history, they never will. My sole contention is that Johnson and Nixon greatly intensified the mistrust.

MR. CORMIER: Working against it, I think, is a great reservoir of goodwill by the people toward presidents. They are willing to put up with an awful lot.

MR. DEAKIN: They keep electing them. Every election of a president reminds me of Dr. Johnson's definition of a second marriage. It is the triumph of hope over experience. We have to have one. They're pretty suspicious, I think, Frank. Obviously you don't feel they're as suspicious as I do. It's a matter of degree, actually.

MS. THOMAS: The people are the last to come around though. I don't think the press deposed Nixon. I think that the people in the end decided he could no longer be believed. And they were the last to come along. When he finally had to admit that he had not told them the truth, that was it. But up to that time, despite one headline after another they still maintained some sort of degree of confidence. And I think that Nixon relied on that. And it was the same way with LBJ. It was only when the people finally took to the streets on the Vietnam war, plus the New Hampshire primary, that he realized he had lost that support.

MR. CORMIER: And he'd had about two or three years of solid support for the war from the American people while most of the press corps certainly, I think, were not in his corner on that.

MS. THOMAS: Exactly.

MR. DEAKIN: One of the things that the press needs to examine and that the public needs to be aware of is that the American public is like any other public. It needs an authority figure. It needs a government. It needs to have its public affairs organized. It needs to believe that there is continuity, that there is stability, that there is hope, all the rest of the things that people have to have in order not to go bonkers. And the press of course exists for an entirely different purpose. There are those academics who maintain, and I agree with them to a considerable extent, that the press helps preserve the legitimacy of our institutions, our political institutions, social institutions, economic institutions. But at the same time, the press is eternally criticizing and finding fault with this authority figure that symbolizes what the American people need in terms of emotional stability and emotional security. The press is doing that, as I am going to be saying this afternoon, simply because that is the way it construes its purpose. That's the way it construes its professionalism, that is what it construes to be its responsibility. If the press just joined in the general approbation, well, history teaches us that it can't join the general approbation because unfortunately if you have nothing but general approbation then you're going to have something very, very bad very quickly. So the press is in constant conflict. The press's findings, what the press covers, the press's quibbling, the press's carping, the press's criticism, the press's uncovering of scandal or mistakes, mostly mistakes above all, is in constant conflict with this emotional need of everybody to have stability and authority. Those two things cannot be reconciled. And they shouldn't be reconciled.

MR. THOMPSON: Is it checks and balances? What underlies this purpose? Is it a fourth branch?

MR. DEAKIN: This involves the professionalism of the press to the extent that you can call it a profession. Some people don't accept that it is a profession. I don't know myself whether it really is. But journalists, I believe, define their professionalism as the pursuit of facts and explanations. Very simple. Well, that just naturally brings them into conflict with all these things, with this need for emotional security, belief in things, with the need for authority, with the need for a secure future. How can you believe in a secure future? How can you believe in authority when the press is constantly telling you the man made a mistake here and the man lied here and the man broke a promise here and he did this bad thing and that bad thing. Of course it's very difficult. It leads the press into conflict.

MS. THOMAS: But it's not the intent to undermine the leader as such. And I don't see. . . .

MR. DEAKIN: That's the question. Does it undermine the leader? Does it undermine the leader of the executive branch that Congress also has power? Does it undermine the president that the Supreme Court frequently overturns legislation, programs, the laws that the president deeply wanted enacted? Was Roosevelt undermined when the Supreme Court threw out the NRA? I think we are losing sight of something here, which is that is that we have set up in this country, including the institution of the press, a whole bunch of built-in conflicts simply to preserve us from despotism. No other reason. And the press is functioning here just as Congress functions. Lyndon Johnson used to say, when he was Senate majority leader, that he wanted to be in on the take-offs as well as the crash landings. He was asserting Congress's insistence that it is a co-equal part of the government. Congress is constantly carping at the president. Congress is constantly criticizing the president. The president, let us say, gets a large majority of his own party in Congress. If he has any experience, he knows he's in trouble because that's the bunch that is going to start taking after him long before the opposition party does. The larger the majority, the harder it is to handle. And Johnson found this, Roosevelt found this, many presidents found it. We have set up a system that is supposed to divide up power so that there won't be despotism, and the press is part of that system. How is it undermined, then? How can it be that it's being undermined? It was set up to be that way.

MS. THOMAS: No, with respect to the press, the whole question of the day-to-day operation is not adversarial. It's exactly "He said," "He added," "He—" whatever the activity was of the day or something. The newspapers are filled with what they would consider positive, of just shoveling the stuff out.

MR. DEAKIN: In other words, as I point out again very briefly in the afternoon talk, basically there are three relationships between the press and the government. I'm talking now of the Washington press corps and the president. There is first what I call the symbiotic relationship, which is what Helen is talking about. Then there is what some people call the adversary relationship, which I don't like as a term but it is in wide use. And then there is the description I prefer, which is the press as a permanent resident critic of government regardless of which party is in power.

Now, in the symbiotic relationship, which as all of you know is the beneficial association of two dissimilar organisms, the press and the president, the press and the government, exist and coexist uneasily. They depend on each other. The president depends on the media for publicity and exposure, and the media depends on the government for, simply, news. Bill Moyers, who has had experience in both, points out that most of the news you see on television unfortunately (and that's Moyers' word, "unfortunately") is what the government says is news, what the government gives out. And Grossman and Kumar—most of you are familiar with the Grossman and Kumar study of the White House press corps and the White House press operation—concluded that despite Vietnam and despite Watergate, which they really considered aberrations, there is more cooperation than conflict. There is more cooperation than conflict between the president and the press. On a day-to-day basis it is a symbiotic relationship, with both of them getting something out of it, and there is a considerable degree of harmony.

It is when you get to issues that are tougher and more important than just routine announcements and housekeeping, to issues that are more embarrassing, that is when you get into the second relationship, which is sometimes called the adversary relationship. I don't like the term and I'd be glad to explain why I don't like it but it's a lengthy kind of thing. And then the third relationship which is what I have been talking about here, the permanent resident critic relationship where the press criticizes regardless of who's in power. I'll be dealing with that in the afternoon speech, too.

MR. THOMPSON: What do any of the three of you say about the argument that the Court and the Congress are appointed or elected and you are not chosen in this way and therefore the analogy with the Congress as a check and balance is a distorted analysis?

MR. DEAKIN: My reply is a phrase that is in very considerable use in this country and has been for a long time. The phrase is: free enterprise. How would you otherwise have it done? Who would appoint the press? The government? The president appoints his cabinet. The president nominates people to the Supreme Court. What would you have the president do? Appoint the editors and reporters, too? How else are you going to do it? The issue we always face in these things was summed up by Winston Churchill, who said that democracy is the worst form of government except all the alternatives. It is very unsatisfactory. But what is the alternative?

MS. THOMAS: I don't understand the premise of your question.

MR. THOMPSON: Well, Doug Cater wrote the book the *Fourth Branch. . . .*

MR. DEAKIN: And all Doug Cater has to do is to tell me who is supposed to appoint the anchormen.

MS. THOMAS: He says that they are not elected or appointed, and therefore they should be—what? Not be influential?

MR. THOMPSON: On the checks and balance issue, Jim has been drawing implied analogies with Congress and the Court. The argument against that view which is often raised is that none of you has been chosen by the people nor are you appointed by officials in the American government. Critics say that for you to see your role as a kind of check and balance within the process is pretentious.

MS. THOMAS: Well, I don't consider it a check. I think it's absolutely indispensable to a democracy. We are the only ones who can question a president, to ever ask him to explain his actions; we don't have a parliamentary system, even Congress cannot basically summon him. Of course it's not an institution of government and it's not in the Constitution *per se,* but how could we ever exist without having a president explain himself, and force him to respond and cross-examine him?

MR. THOMPSON: Is it like the question period? If you say it is don't you get into another questionable analogy, namely, whether press conferences are anything like the question period?

MR. CORMIER: It's a very inadequate substitute for it, I think. Our questioning role is so evanescent and it's here today and gone tomorrow, when the man goes into hiding for three months as they do occasionally.

MR. DEAKIN: Not regularly. It's not really regularized.

MR. CORMIER: No, there's nothing regular about it.

MR. DEAKIN: That's not our fault.

MS. THOMAS: But it is still the only place where you can actually, by public pressure and public opinion, force a president to explain himself. Because they can build up or go for five or six months without a news conference but when you start writing that people realize that he is obviously hiding out, as Nixon did during the Watergate era when he went for five months without one.

MR. DEAKIN: At the end, it was five months between press conferences. But that was during the Time of the Great Trouble.

MS. THOMAS: But he only had three in 1974 before he resigned and he resigned in August.

MR. DEAKIN: He held thirty-nine press conferences in five and a half years. That comes out to one-half press conference per month, which is not possible except arithmetically. But although he only held thirty-nine press conferences in five and a half years, an average of less than about one half press conference per month compared to Roosevelt's six press conferences per month, before he had been in office one year, one full year, he was on national television fourteen times.

Now, the point I'd like to make about what Helen is saying is that the press conference is not only a substitute for the question period in the House of the Commons; it is also almost the only two-way communication the American people have with their president. Those fourteen times Nixon was on television in the first year were one-way communications. If you didn't like what he was saying or you didn't agree with it, you had only certain alternatives and none of them involved two-way communication. You could switch to another channel and there was Nixon again. Or you could turn it off. Or you could throw something at it—beer cans were the favorite. That's it. If you didn't agree with something he was saying or you didn't think he was giving a full explanation, if you thought he was leaving something out, you had no way of communicating that to Richard Nixon. You could shout at the TV set, but he did not hear you.

MS. THOMAS: You could write a letter or call the White House.

MR. DEAKIN: But when there is a press conference and reporters are asking questions, he has to listen. He hears what they are saying.

MR. CORMIER: But do you judge press conferences as being two-way?

MS. THOMAS: Yes. I do.

MR. DEAKIN: As inadequate and as incomplete as they are, and as limited and with all their faults, yes.

MS. THOMAS: Closer than watching television.

MR. CORMIER: Closer than watching television, yes. But I'd like to see someone do a study on the percentage of basically non-responsive answers to press conference questions because I think it's quite high.

MS. THOMAS: The American people can tell an artful dodge. That in itself is telling us something.

MR. THOMPSON: What about Carter's grass roots town meetings and the like?

MR. DEAKIN: Let's talk about that. People say, well, Carter tried to get two-way communication by going out and talking to the American people, holding town meetings and so forth. A good deal of the time at the town meetings was taken up by people asking the President of the United States what he was going to do about the sewage disposal plant in their community. This did not add to the enlightenment or the information of the American people on the broad major issues facing them. A great deal of time was taken up with questions that were not informative to the nation as a whole. They were things like what are you doing about the pot holes here in Centerville?

MS. THOMAS: Good public relations.

MR. DEAKIN: Good public relations, but it was not really two-way communication. That was the first thing. The second thing was that they did ask him some good questions, and I have no objection whatever to the president holding these meetings—I'm in favor of two-way communication no matter how he does it: press conferences, town meetings or visits to the homes of the poor, if the poor are not so awed by it that they forget to ask how come you cut off my welfare. But the quintessential example of the presidential trip or town meeting as a form of two-way communication with the American people was Carter's trip on the steamboat. He took his vacation on a steamboat and went down the Mississippi, and he would get off at certain places and mingle with the public to get the feel of how they were doing. So he got off at one place and he approached a likely-looking citizen and asked him what he thought about some major problem in foreign affairs. And the poor man was absolutely baffled. He said, "Mr. President, I don't know anything about that. I'm a window washer. Do you have any windows in the White House that need washing?" Fine, but it just doesn't add to the information of the American people.

MS. THOMAS: We do—any time the president wants to communicate and to be interrogated, whether it's at a town meeting, we'll go for that but we don't want it to replace the press conference, which they tried to do.

MR. JONES: I'm very interested in your comments about press secretaries and the almost personal nature of the comments. But I conclude, at least the ones who are post-Hagerty, that they don't sound very formidable, almost hardly a contest in this business of the conflicting purposes as you define them between the presidency and the press. Are your remarks to be interpreted as a desire for a stronger foe or for none at all so that you might elevate the contest?

MR. DEAKIN: We look at each of these press secretaries from several standpoints. One, how well-informed they are. That in turn depends almost completely on their relationship with the president, how much he tells them, and more important, how much he has the senior staff tell them, whether he lets them into the senior staff meetings, whether the senior staff views the press secretary as an equal or just a subordinate functionary. This is vital. It is vital not just to the press but to the American people that the press secretary know something, that he have some information. He can only get that information under two circumstances. One, if he is himself a very forceful personality and insists that he be told. Or, two, he has a relationship with the president whereby the senior staff know that they can't conceal things from the press secretary. Those are the only two ways, really, that he can get information. He can get it himself if he's very forceful or he gets it from the senior staff because the senior staff knows the president wants him to have it. So this is what the press needs most, a well-informed press secretary.

Then beyond that, there is the problem of quality and quantity. What the press wants is access. Access is the life blood of the reporter. Can he get to people, will they talk to him? At the White House, that starts with the press secretary; it goes beyond the press secretary, but it starts with him. First, you have to have quantity of access. Do you have frequent briefings and press conferences? Quantity. You have to have quantity of access, but equally important is the *quality* of the access. Once the press secretary is up there holding his briefing, does he know anything? Has he enough standing with the president that he can tell things to the reporters without fear? In other words, quality, the quality of the access. If he stonewalls day in and day out, if he's afraid of his own shadow, if he will not talk, if he's afraid of the president, if he's afraid of the senior staff, we get nothing. And we have contempt for him. And we know right away, the press knows right away, what the relationship is between the press secretary and the president.

MR. JONES: And it really has created that kind of press secretary, this type that has a stake in creating distance, and that type makes the job more difficult because you have to deal with whatever is given out. And so the public in a sense hears something that may not be the case and so you've got to break through that first. That's your point. And it would be better not to have them at all.

MR. DEAKIN: Well, there have been times, and I think maybe Helen would agree with me, possibly Frank, there have been times when things have got so bad in the briefings that I have made a mental resolve that I was going to stop going because it was such a waste of time. Helen and Frank couldn't take that position. The wire services have to be there. But I'm sure they have often felt . . .

MR. CORMIER: I took a nap occasionally.

MR. DEAKIN: But you end up continuing to go for two reasons. I'm talking about a "special" now, not a wire service reporter, a "special" working for one newspaper. You keep going for two reasons. One, just to keep track of the housekeeping details: when is he going to go on a trip, when he is leaving, when is this message coming out, you know—the logistics and housekeeping stuff. And the second, and this can be valuable, you go for the atmosphere, for the osmosis. How do the other reporters feel about the experiences they're having? There's a feel around that place if you're there a long time, and it becomes very important to keep that feel current. You hear things here, there, and the other place. Some secretary may say something or drop something, and another reporter may have heard something. A lot of it is gossip, but a lot of it is osmotic information that you're just sort of getting through your pores. And so you keep going. But often the material, the quality of the material coming out of the briefing, it's just not there.

MS. THOMAS: We're not looking for a stronger foe. Far from it. We don't think we should be foes.

MR. DEAKIN: We're just looking for information. We only have one thing in mind, facts and explanations, that's all. There's no conspiracy.

MS. THOMAS: And nothing do they resent more.

MR. BLACKFORD: You may recall that a rumor was planted by the Nixon White House, the day that Jerry Ford was named vice president, to the effect that Linwood Holton was going to be named vice president. I'm glad that rumor didn't turn out to be true.

MR. CORMIER: That was a Johnson type maneuver.

MR. BLACKFORD: Well, Carroll Kilpatrick called somebody at the *Post* on it, and the *Post* actually did go into type with that. The world was calling me as Holton's press secretary at seven-thirty at night for information and I'm saying there isn't a word of truth in this.

MR. DEAKIN: You were not only denying the allegation, you were denying the alligator.

MR. BLACKFORD: I would like to make a few comments if you don't mind because, in retrospect, I feel extremely fortunate. Number one, I am a member of what I call the IWNMM club, that is the "I was a newspaper man myself," and I define journalism as something Jefferson said, which is "For here we are not afraid to follow the truth wherever it may lead nor to tolerate error so long as reason is left free to combat it." But, from my own experience let me make just one or two comments. Holton got hold of me in the spring of 1969 and said he wanted to get somebody who knew the working press of Virginia but he didn't want just an ordinary flack, that he wanted to set up a brains trust and that I would be in on all the big decisions and what not if he was elected. And this promise he kept. And indeed I had a unique responsibility for a press secretary. Holton was a great delegator of authority. And as it turned out, I didn't know this when I took the job or I might have hesitated. I became his speech writer as well as his press secretary. And with the exception of the State of the State messages, that first couple of weeks in office I'd go in and say, "You've got to make such and such a speech, now what do you want to talk about?" And he said, "You take care of it." So in effect, in this important aspect of the administration, I wrote speeches. I knew the way Holton talked, we were sort of alike and both of us were particularly concerned about the racial question. I had been with the Southern Council in Atlanta before coming back to Virginia as a newspaper man.

The other point I want to make is that the Governor generally did like reporters and he was not afraid of them. And this made things a lot easier. And he had a good sense of humor. He didn't try to mislead the press, as far as I know. I can't remember any instance of that.

And I'd like finally to say my favorite story of the Holton years involves one other anecdote. He acquired a tough skin but this was not due to me, it was due to a great Virginian named Colgate Darden. Early in his administration, even before he got into problems about school desegregation, he tried to raise a tobacco tax in Virginia. Well, that was like knocking down the sacred Ark of Delphi in Richmond. The *Richmond Times Dispatch* had an editorial rather critical of him. The man he consulted with throughout his administration was a man named Colgate Darden. Holton was concerned about this editorial in the *Times Dispatch* and Mr. Darden said, "Governor, there's only one way you can please the Richmond newspapers." And Holton said, "How's that?" He replied, "What you've got to do is you've got to come out and advocate a return to slavery and do it under conditions they can understand."

MR. CORMIER: In other words, keep it simple. Terrific.

MR. BLACKFORD: Finally, I want to end up with an anecdote. In the fall of 1973, I was down in the Capitol press room and a reporter was talking to other reporters in the news room about the Holton administration. And the reporter, then of the *Richmond News Leader*, said, "Well, Holton had more fun than any man that's ever been governor." And another reporter who was with the Associated Press said, "Yes, and that's the reason the rest of us had so much fun." That probably wouldn't happen at the national level.

MS. THOMAS: No, I think it would. Why not?

MR. DEAKIN: We had a lot of fun with Kennedy. It's a great help if the president has a sense of humor, and it's a great help if he's a secure man.

MS. THOMAS: Exactly.

MR. DEAKIN: But secure men do not get elected to top national office all that often.

MR. LATIMER: If you became President tomorrow, whom would you appoint as your press secretary?

MR. DEAKIN: I'd handle it like Kennedy. I'd try to be my own press secretary to the greatest extent possible, and then I would find a really good wire service or newspaper reporter to handle it when I couldn't.

MR. CORMIER: The nuts and bolts.

MR. DEAKIN: The nuts and bolts, yes.

MR. THOMPSON: The symbiotic part?

MR. DEAKIN: The symbiotic part, by and large.

MR. LATIMER: My second question is a little bit irrelevant. What is Bill Moyers up to? What is he running for?

MR. DEAKIN: You saw the Dave Broder column, didn't you, where he was matching off Jim Baker and Moyers, saying that they both want to be president? Well, I hope we have a chance either during Helen's or Frank's presentation to get into this whole question, because television and the power struggle between television and government now is at such a level of national importance that to some extent the old rules are off. Newspapers have always fought with presidents but no newspaper has ever had the influence and the pervasiveness of television. In its finest hour, no newspaper ever reached the people that television is reaching. So you have to ask yourself, it seems to me, an extremely important question. Let's use Moyers only as a symbol because there are some others on television who do this. But CBS is the network that does it the most often, these specials on "Hunger in America" or "The Selling of the Pentagon" or the Alaskan gas pipeline financing or this latest one, "People Like Us," where they are obviously raising the most serious questions about something that an administration is doing. And you have to ask yourself, are they doing this as a power struggle with the government, where they wish to prevail, just as the government wishes to prevail, or are they simply covering a story? Are they functioning as journalists covering a story? Now, Moyers with his unemployment story, was Moyers simply covering unemployment? Or if you want to go all the way back to Murrow, was Murrow simply covering Joseph R. McCarthy in that famous broadcast, or was he having a power struggle with McCarthy? Was he trying to destroy McCarthy? And the only conceivable answer, of course, is both. Both are going on. Moyers is covering a story, the story of unemployment. And he's covering it the way television covers it, very dramatically, in very human terms, because television can only deal in human terms. It has to be something you can make a movie out of. Television can't show you an interest rate rising. It can only show you people and what they're saying.

MS. THOMAS: What's motivating your question? You think he's doing more than his job, obviously.

MR. LATIMER: I'm sorry, I did not see the famous telecast; I'd read about it and I was just curious.

MS. THOMAS: And when you say "up to" though, why wouldn't he be doing a documentary on the subject?

MR. LATIMER: I had read the gossip that he might be running for senator or president or something. That's what I meant.

MR. DEAKIN: Every now and then you hear a report that somebody in the media, someone who has become very well known by virtue of being on television, is running for office.

MR. CORMIER: Did Chet Huntley run for senator?

MR. DEAKIN: The one I'm thinking of is Marvin Kalb. They started a movement for him to run for the Senate from Maryland, remember that? Most of the time, journalists skitter away from it. My own theory is that journalists are too self-conscious to be politicians, literally too self-conscious about what they're saying. They just cannot put out the same kind of talk that politicians put out. They can't do that kind of equivocation. They can't make those promises and so forth. So it's remarkable, considering the influence of journalism, it's remarkable how few journalists in this country, even today in television, go into politics. Very few. Consider, for instance, doctors. Now, doctors obviously have much less connection with politics than journalists, but there are usually a number of doctors in Congress. But very few journalists. If they were tempermentally politicians they would be politicians, not journalists. And they're not. So Helen, obviously, from her reaction to your question, is saying no, she thinks Bill Moyers was just doing the journalist's job of covering a news story. Unemployment is a news story right now.

MS. THOMAS: Well, I don't know. He may have hidden ambitions.

MR. DEAKIN: I'm taking the position that he's covering a news story but because television is what it is, because it is so pervasive and so powerful, inevitably it takes on the aura or the aspect of a power struggle also.

MS. THOMAS: And that's what it became actually in terms of that particular broadcast. They try to block everything almost—not to block it but to get equal time. And even before it went on they were afraid that it would be very damaging.

MR. DEAKIN: Because the White House knew the kind of damage that was being done to it, so of course they want equal time. It wouldn't surprise me to see Bill Moyers run for president. But the reason he would be running for president would be because he started out in government, not because he's in journalism now. He has some political feeling.

MR. CORMIER: I'd be surprised to see him run. But I might not be surprised if he tried.

MS. THOMAS: President Johnson complained that Moyers wanted to be the president, that he was acting like he was President.

MR. CORMIER: Well, they had a very bitter falling out.

MR. DEAKIN: Well, Johnson bad-mouthed everybody when they left. He hated that.

MR. CORMIER: Yes. And he never saw Moyers again. He wouldn't see him.

MS. THOMAS: He thought he was plotting with Bobby Kennedy.

MR. DEAKIN: Moyers resigned. He wasn't fired. Moyers resigned and Johnson used to tell us, "That's why I fired Moyers and Bundy. They held too many backgrounders." Remember that? He didn't fire either one of them, but after they left he decided he had fired them.

MS. THOMAS: Well, I think he eased out Moyers, though. One thing when he was getting rid of people he always tried to make sure that they got big hundred thousand dollar jobs.

MR. BLACKFORD: If he got rid of a secretary he made sure she had an eligible catch.

MS. THOMAS: Right. Exactly.

MR. DEAKIN: But that was only if they hadn't had a falling out. If they had a falling out he wouldn't lift a finger.

MS. THOMAS: No, he had never forgiven Reedy. Reedy was the only one, I think, not invited to the library dedication.

MR. DEAKIN: Yes, I remember that. That was a horrible thing because Reedy had served this man with consummate loyalty.

MS. THOMAS: He couldn't stand the *Twilight of the Presidency.*

MR. DEAKIN: But Johnson was an extremely insecure man. Unbelievable. He didn't look like it but he was a frightened man. Now, this is psyching the president. There's a big argument in journalism whether we should psychoanalyze the president. A lot of journalists say that's not our business and we shouldn't do it. But inevitably you find yourself psyching the president. You can't help it.

MS. THOMAS: I think you psych them before. You try to figure out what manner of president they'll be.

MR. DEAKIN: Yes. Part of it's legitimate because we're trying to figure out what he'll do in given situations, and the personality is part of that.

MR. BLACKFORD: Would you agree that if he hadn't gotten mixed up in Vietnam he probably would have been remembered as one of the greatest presidents?

MR. DEAKIN: Oh, I don't think there's any question of that.

MS. THOMAS: I think he'll still go down as one of the greatest.

RONALD REAGAN AND THE
MANAGEMENT OF THE NEWS

Helen Thomas

MR. THOMPSON: I want to read a bit from someone who very early in the Reagan administration wrote the following column:

> President Reagan has managed to keep his domestic program of massive federal spending cuts on center stage but in the foreign policy field he still is feeling his way. The policy so far has been marked by ambiguities and contradictions with no apparent overall direction. The current line vis-à-vis the Soviets appears to be the hallmark but even that seems vulnerable to other pragmatic requirements.

That piece written by Helen Thomas stands up rather well.

Helen Thomas was born in Kentucky; attended Wayne University; has honorary degrees from a number of institutions; served as wire service reporter in Washington beginning in 1943; White House bureau chief, 1974 to the present; was president of the White House Correspondents Association, 1975-76, the first woman president; was the recipient of the Woman of the Year in Communications Award by the *Ladies Home Journal*; was the first woman elected to the Gridiron Club of Washington; has been a member of the Women's National Press Corps and its president; has been a member of Sigma Delta Chi's Hall of Fame; Delta Sigma Pi's honorary membership; is the author of *Dateline: White House* and, finally, is one of the most respected figures in the American field of journalism. It's a privilege to welcome you to Virginia.

MS. THOMAS: I'm honored to be here at the University founded by a great defender of freedom of the press, Thomas Jefferson, though he may have wondered himself at times what hath God wrought. I'm particularly proud to be on the same platform with two great reporters who know so well the byzantine manipulation of information at the White House through the years. For as all presidents learn, information equals power. Press relations with any president always run a predictable course—downhill. And it may be ever thus as long as we are the watchmen at the tower.

I've always considered myself greatly privileged to cover the White House. Each day is an education and of course we have the proverbial ringside to history, instant history. It's true, of course, inasmuch as some may think otherwise, we are mindful that human beings live in the White House with their joys, their sorrows, their insecurities, their arrogance and their rare nobility. The obvious inevitable prognosis for relations between any president and the press seems to go from bad to worse, though not in the beginning when every president is accorded a honeymoon. That was best typified when the *Washington Post* cartoonist, Herblock, gave Nixon a clean shave after he assumed office. Many years earlier dating back to the McCarthy era, he drew Nixon in the most sinister terms. In the full flush of an inauguration presidents are twelve feet tall and all is right with the world. The press, too, is caught up in this uncritical moment that goes along with learning that, in those first euphoric days of Gerald Ford's accession, Ford toasted his own English muffins. Then there is the mood, perhaps in the press as well as the country, to give him a chance as his style and his actions come into focus.

Ronald Reagan had a longer honeymoon than most presidents. The attempt on his life coming so soon after he had moved into the White House produced an understandable brief moratorium and bought him some time, even as his aides spoke of a "safety net for the poor" as social programs were being slashed. As time went on, the press was accused of not laying a glove on Reagan and some of their peers like Anthony Lewis wrote that reporters were being too soft on the President and were giving him a free ride. Since we see ourselves as factual reporters, I don't think a day has passed that we have not faithfully reported Reagan's moves to dismantle the programs from the New Deal to the Great Society, or at least to curb them radically. From that aspect Reagan has been true to his philosophy. He is a rigid ideologue and only rarely does he beat a strategic retreat.

In the early days of the Reagan administration the promise was, as it is with every president, an open administration. I can only say—that will be the day, not only for this administration, but all the others we've covered. Press access to Reagan during his 1980 campaign was extremely limited, more a case of hit-and-run with aides closing in before a reporter could toss a follow-up question. The *modus operandi* continued at the White House. Then reporters were treated to an affable, genial, nice president—very friendly, seemingly willing to answer any question during brief so-called photo opportunities in the Oval Office. His top aides, Edwin Meese, James Baker, Michael Deaver, all neophytes to the national government—except Baker whose own experience was limited—became apopleptic when Reagan would deliver an off-the-cuff answer. Reagan himself could not resist an answer. But it appeared that his aides protectively and perhaps with some smug superiority on their part felt that he should not be questioned, that they were really smarter than he was and that some of his answers were not programmed or screened enough.

Since the picture takings were the only point of access to Reagan, reporters tried to make the most of it. I recall one day when Reagan was meeting with a head of state, the "thundering herd," which is what we're called, rushed into the Oval Office. The time was ten forty-five a.m., fifteen minutes before the eleven o'clock deadline that Reagan had set for firing the air traffic controllers. It was an opportunity not to be passed up. I asked Reagan while picture-taking was going on if he was indeed going ahead with his plan to fire the controllers. He said he was and we ran to our electronic computers, not the telephone as often any more. Within hours his top aides decided that they had had it with impromptu questions to the press and they laid down the law that Reagan was not to be questioned when he was with a foreign leader for decorum's sake. We agreed to nothing and never do, but we did not push our luck with heads of state. Then, heady with a bit of success in putting us in our place, the Reaganites decided that all questions to the President during such sessions should be verbotten. We defy those rules all the time but in their frustration they devised a system whereby once a week Reagan would answer questions in a quicky ten minute encounter on their own terms and whenever they decide.

Access to Reagan is very limited and under the most controlled circumstances. He's had nine news conferences so far, a far cry from FDR and some of his predecessors. FDR held two a week even in wartime. Being human, presidents do not relish the idea of meeting the press, particularly when there's nothing to brag about. When Jim Brady was on deck, he managed to keep the atmosphere light and to deflect hostility. It no longer is the Gulag that we once knew in the Nixon era. His deputy, Larry Speakes, who presides at news briefings came up through a tough school. He had worked in the White House in the Nixon era as spokesman for Nixon's chief Watergate lawyer.

Speakes, White House Communications Director David Gergen, and the big three advisors huddle every day to decide what story they will feature, what story will land Reagan on the front page in the best light, of course. They decide what activity of the day involving the President we can cover. Days can go by when we do not see him, even when he has a full official schedule on the record. The term "managed news" coined in the Kennedy era has been developed to a fine art. Reagan's aides even have trained him to say, "I can't comment, it's a photo opportunity." It's all on their terms and they calculate what will do them the most good, imagewise.

And yet one wonders at times, because sometimes it gets away from them. For example, last Friday when the highest unemployment rate since the Great Depression was announced, Reagan, togged out in his lovely riding britches, came out on the South Lawn, denounced the Democrats for demagoguery and went off like the playboy of the western world on a helicopter to go riding in the Virginia countryside. And then he was very stubborn image-wise when his aides told him that the economy was so bad and the picture was so bad that he really shouldn't take a vacation in Barbados and stay at the home of Claudette Colbert seeming to be wallowing in the rich atmosphere that he's often identified with. He insisted that he was going, so they immediately started putting on some official meetings, had him stop overnight in Jamaica where he could be treated as a head of state and have official talks on the Caribbean. Then, when he went to Barbados, they did have a meeting with some of the smaller Caribbean nation leaders. Then for three days he had his vacation. Well, the AP, unfortunately not us, did the story saying that it cost the taxpayers 3.5 million dollars for Reagan to have his vacation in the Barbados, which he insisted on doing even though his aides had told him, imagewise, it's not so good. Then he made a speech, one of his regular Saturday radio speeches and he started out by saying, "Well, I took the day off on Good Friday like everyone takes off and I'm going to church on Sunday," and it was so defensive. But he did have his vacation. It isn't "Let them eat cake," but I think that he calls his own shots even though they try to manage and program him.

In recent months Reagan has lost some of his initial affability with the press. But not all. He has fallen into the presidential syndrome of displaying anger over leaks from time to time. Washington is one giant ear, he has complained. He also says he is convinced there are bugs in the chandelier in the cabinet room. Many of the reforms that grew out of the nightmare that was Watergate have been eliminated or will be if Reagan has his way. The drive has been systematic to cut down legitimate access to news in the foreign policy field. New regulations have been devised to tighten the circle of those with access to top secret documents. The Freedom of Information Act is under siege, and Reagan's forces seek to legitimatize domestic spying by the CIA.

Worse yet is the atmosphere of darkness at noon with lie detectors being used to nail the leakers. When a colonel was accused of leaking the report that experts believed that defense spending would rise dramatically to a trillion dollars, he was informed that he would probably lose his job, although it's still under investigation. "We want to make an example of him," said one Pentagon spokesman. *Deja vu.* No plumbers on the scene so far as we can tell. But the atmosphere is conducive. There is little or no room for devil's advocates in this administration and it's doubtful that Reagan gets a variety of opinion except for the bickering that was often exposed between then Secretary of State Alexander Haig and Defense Secretary Caspar Weinberger. The people are not in on the take-offs, only the landings.

I remember when they started the whole focus on El Salvador. Ed Meese appeared on "Issues and Answers." It was February, one month after Reagan had taken office and we were practically drawing a line in El Salvador. People didn't know what was going to happen next. And Meese went on the air and under questioning said, "We will do whatever is necessary in El Salvador." And we heard this program had been taped so he got on Air Force One with us coming back from Santa Barbara to Washington; he came back to the press area and we said, "What do you mean, whatever is necessary? What exactly? Will you be a little more specific?" And I said, "After all, when do the American people enter into this dialogue on what is our foreign policy, and whether they fight and not?" He said, "They come in every four years when they elect a president."

MR. CORMIER: A lot can happen in four years.

MS. THOMAS: The people's right to know is coming under attack by some elitists in the press and the press is always under attack. But we know too well how much is suppressed under the stamp of national security, and the price of such secrecy. Exposure of the bombing of Cambodia for fourteen months in the *New York Times* sent Nixon and Henry Kissinger up in smoke, and spotlighted their long deception in that Vietnam war and other war moves.

Of course the lack of credibility at that time was not restricted to Nixon. The Johnson era is replete with such stories. Reporters will not soon forget Secretary of State Dean Rusk, angered over the line of questioning on the Vietnam war, asked reporters, "Which side are you on? I'm on our side," he said. Inevitably, it becomes a matter of self-protection for those running the show, badly or not. And then there was the Kennedy era when Pentagon spokesman Arthur Sylvester contended that the government had the right to lie in national security matters. I saw two presidents bite the dust because they were no longer believed, and without credibility they could not govern: Lyndon Johnson and Richard Nixon. And it was not without some incredulity that I watched six press secretaries take brief nostalgic turns at bat at the White House podium recently. All but one, Jody Powell, maintained that they had never lied to the press. Ron Nessen did admit that he had deceived the press on one occasion as to the reason why President Ford wanted to take a trip to Florida. Later he said it was for a golf match. Powell couched his only fib in the cloak of national security, naturally. He said he had lied about the ill-fated hostage rescue mission in Iran. Unfortunately, I did not have a Bible on hand to rush up to them and ask them to play it again and raise your right hand.

I do not, and never have, underestimated the difficulty of speaking for a president. Few have ever done it well and it can only be with fear and trepidation. And then there are people like LBJ who could hardly stand having a White House mouthpiece. As a consequence he had five of them and none excelled at the job. LBJ was his own press secretary for better or for worse. My ideal press secretary wears two hats. He is indeed the voice of the White House but he also has a responsibility to keep the American people informed and to maintain the accountability of a president. Few have filled the bill well. Perhaps James Hagerty for Eisenhower was above par; Pierre Salinger was good for Kennedy because he was tuned in, and for one brief shining month we had Jerry ter Horst for Ford. He quit when he was deceived in the White House about the Nixon pardon. I think it should also be remembered that press secretaries are paid by the taxpayer. They are government servants not to be confused with publicists hired to do a public relations job for the president, even though they don't see it that way.

And then there is the image. Reagan has been appalled and admits being very disturbed over the perception that he is Scrooge, cutting school milk and food stamp programs, college tuition loans, disability, and so on. He has become particularly irate when the television networks feature programs about the poor, victims of cuts in benefits. "Anytime anyone gets laid off in South Succotash he gets interviewed on television," Reagan complained. Counselor Edwin Meese at the Sperling breakfast accused the networks of running up and down the street trying to find someone out of work to portray the bad effects of

Reaganomics. "TV reporting is so downbeat it is hurting the economic recovery," says Reagan. But their complaints do not hold water. Reagan cannot say that he does not get ample television exposure anytime he chooses. As for his advisors, turn on any TV any morning and especially on Sunday talk shows and try not to find one of them being interviewed on the major network programs.

Like his predecessors, Reagan has found late Friday afternoon, when there are few reporters around, is just the right time to drop the touchy news such as financial disclosure statements of top aides on the table, and income tax returns. And when it came time to reveal Reagan's order to the IRS to give tax exemptions to schools with known discriminatory policies, of course it was put out late Friday. Every day the White House turns out a bunch of releases, mostly appointments, including U.S. marshals, for various reasons. Trivia for most reporters but for wire services we do carry them because we are covering the whole country. Yet, when the administration decided to ask Congress for a new multi-billion dollar civil defense program, it was released by the Federal Emergency Management Agency, put out on a quiet wire without any fanfare with only alert reporters finally catching up. One has to ask why. Surely a program affecting the safety of every American should have been announced at the White House. But perhaps the White House wanted no close identity with a program that informs Americans that they've got eight days to get out of town in the event of a nuclear war.

I know that in the eyes of some the role of the press is dubious. We are self-appointed watchdogs, annointed by none, feared by some, and guided, we hope, by one main ethical goal: to pursue the truth wherever it leads. If government servants are watched, well, we are, too. We reporters get a report card every day. Every day we are tested for our accuracy and our profound responsibility to the American people. And I must say that there would be no covering of the White House if the White House didn't have a lot of rope. People will never know how physical is such a job and how demeaning in many ways because we never cover a president except when they put a rope around us. We're corralled like cattle. The Secret Service now has taken over our lives in the protection of the president, whether valid or not. More and more they've discovered helicopters—he rarely travels in public, his access to people has become almost nonexistent except on occasion when everything is very sanitized.

But the whole question is that reporters are some sort of a necessity yet this is the way we are treated. Our credibility is also at stake and is much more quickly exposed for all to see in any newspapers, on any television. A Supreme Court Justice once said that a constant spotlight on public officials lessens the possibility of corruption. And in the words of Justice Brandeis, if the government becomes a law breaker, it breeds contempt for the law. The importance of a free and robust press cannot be underestimated, but that we are a thorn in the side of government officials and others in public life is obvious. We know it's not our role to be loved or even liked—respected, we hope, and even by presidents, for being fair.

Each president has had his troubles with the press, going back to George Washington. We have a photograph of FDR in our press room which is inscribed to the White House reporters from their "devoted victim." "When the press stops abusing me, I'll know I'm in the wrong pew," said Truman. "Reading more and enjoying it less," said Kennedy. What LBJ said is unprintable. Nixon had his enemy's list and, once when the press walked into the cabinet room for picture taking, Nixon looked up at the press and said, "It's only coincidental that we're talking about pollution when the press walks in." Carter always seemed to be saying, "Lord, forgive them, for they know not what they do." As for Reagan, well, it's like being in those silent movies. He thinks we should be seen and not heard.

But I thought that Amy Carter kind of summed up the attitude when her mother escorted her to a public school, first day in class after they moved into the White House. Reporters and cameramen had been alerted in Washington that they could record this historic moment and promise never to bother little Amy again. And so the reporters and photographers flanked the walk to the school door. Amy looked at the press, her hand was held by her mother and she looked up at her mother and said, "Mom, do we still have to be nice to them?"

And I'll go with Jeff Carter, the former President's youngest son during the first Christmas in Plains, Georgia. We were standing across the street from the family home keeping an eye on Carter who had come out on the porch, playing with his grandchildren, grandstanding, we thought, on the porch for our benefit. A television cameraman asked Jeff, who strolled across the street, if he didn't feel sorry for his father hounded by the press, clocking his every move, and Jeff said, "No, he asked for it." And I guess that's the way I feel about presidents. They ask for it, knowing the press tries to be ever vigilant, ever present to keep an eye on the person who has life and death, push-button power over all humanity today, to keep the people informed and democracy alive. Thank you.

MR. THOMPSON: Do you think it's numbers that threaten presidents? If there were not as many reporters following them, if there were three of you, say, or ten more, would some of these historic attitudes of aversion toward the press be as deep-seated?

MS. THOMAS: You mean in terms of how we're treated?

MR. THOMPSON: Well, yes, and in terms of the negative attitudes toward the press.

MS. THOMAS: In terms of the public or the White House?

MR. THOMPSON: Well, in the early press conference days people talked about the fact that Roosevelt could fit the reporters into the Oval Office. Now if a graduate student at American University has made a contribution to President Carter's campaign he can get into a press conference.

MS. THOMAS: I don't think there's any question that the magnitude of the press corps now magnifies the problem. But I maintain that sometimes when we're only a pool of three or four reporters the Secret Service still continues to push us around because it's become a built-in syndrome. You cannot believe that if you're wearing a pass, if you have been cleared by the Secret Service, that you shouldn't even be in the White House if you're any kind of threat, and yet they continue to draw a line on every step you take.

MR. LATIMER: Did that then accentuate during the Reagan administration or was it just as bad under Carter and the others?

MS. THOMAS: It gave the Secret Service a chance for a quantum leap. They would just as soon keep him in a little capsule and. . . .

MR. DEAKIN: What you're saying is that this jump started after the assassination attempt?

MR. LATIMER: That's what I was wondering.

MS. THOMAS: It's all relative.

MR. CORMIER: It was not to this degree by any means, not at all.

MR. LATIMER: Does this seem to be the personal decision by Reagan himself? I mean, if left to his own devices would he do all this?

MS. THOMAS: Oh no, no. He's a friendly, nice man. There is no question about it. He likes people; I think he perhaps is not as affable as sometimes he appears but he certainly is a good politician. He knows people are important to a politician. But of course the press is in the role that you can't defy security because, indeed, they may be right or maybe they know something you don't know. But I am saying that people will never understand what it takes to get information. One day I was on a helicopter six times just covering the President to make sure that while he is in public nothing happens. I know it's macabre but that's the way it goes.

MR. CORMIER: It goes to ridiculous lengths. This is almost off the point but I can't forget it. Paul Healy borrowed a book from Nelson

Rockefeller when he was vice president and the security in the old Executive Office Building in Washington, at least prior to Reagan, was much more stringent than at the White House. And so Paul had an appointment to see Rockefeller to return this book. The police stopped him, wanted to know what he was doing and he explained, and they made a call to Rockefeller's office: yes, he had the appointment; and the police said, "You can go in but the book stays here." It becomes pretty damn oppressive.

MS. THOMAS: At the same time the press offices also do not want us to comment—well, in terms of image this is a very interesting thing. You're always challenged on your own scepticism. Are you being fair? Every reporter does the same soulsearching every day. I've seen the Reagan administration make many end runs around civil rights laws, trying to cut them down and so forth. There's no question about it. Then the President picked up the newspaper, as they tell it later, and reads about this one family in College Park, Maryland right outside of Washington that had been harrassed; they've had a cross burning five years ago, crank telephone calls and garbage dumped on their lawn. He is struck by this horror and he comes in waving his newspaper in the Oval Office and he asks his aide, "What can we do about this? This is terrible, I'd like to go see them."

So the aide proceeds to put everything in place, get in touch with the family's lawyer and so forth and six hours later Larry Speakes comes running out. We have fifteen minutes to get on a helicopter because the President's going to go visit this family. He says the President did not want to take any press with him. He just wants to go tell this family how sorry he is, but we have talked him into having the press there— with the four thirty and the six o'clock news, you've got an hour and a half to make good—but we insisted, we told him that he had to. So anyway the President gets on the helicopter on the South Lawn and we go practically to the Washington Monument to get on another helicopter, fly to another spot, motorcade through the rush hour to get to this family. The President and Mrs. Reagan go into this home to talk to the family. The family had been alerted, the little girl was in her Sunday best and so forth. Every neighbor—I mean, at least 150 neighbors who were supposed to be maltreating these people and I'm sure they had been—were there, every television station had sent a cameraman and reporter. It's a good local story as well as for us, it was very good. But three or four times we were told the President absolutely did not want any press but that they had convinced him that it was necessary because he would be in public. He spends about 20 minutes inside the house, then comes out and a reporter asks a question, He is from here to the wall and one of his aides said "No further, this is the line." This is Andersonville. They drew the line. We were part of a pool, we had traveled with him and so forth. So you still find yourself almost shouting and he obviously wants to talk.

Then I think: am I so cynical that I think that maybe they wanted the press? They are embarked on an image change in terms of blacks, women, whatever and yet, I said, maybe he legitimately did not want the press, so you are confused as to where the truth is. Anyway, my feelings did not get into my story. I wrote it as factually as possible, pulling out all the stops on how the neighbors felt and so forth. Reporters do their own soul searching and I'm a cynic with hope.

Well, they did make the evening news, indeed they did in a very positive way.

MR. DEAKIN: Can I make a comment on the subject of bigness? What you're really asking, I gather, is: Are the American people offended and do they grow irritated and suspicious when they see this tremendous quantity of coverage, the number of people surrounding the president? You've got television people and cameras, and the president and the press are all jockeying for position and so forth. In a way you dealt with this in your commission report—the shouting, the waving hands and so forth.

Two points: In 1937, when Leo Rosten wrote his book on the Washington press corps, he found that there were six hundred accredited correspondents in Washington. He did this simply by counting up the number of reporters and photographers who were accredited to the Congressional press galleries. Today the figure is at least 4,300. So the press corps between 1937 and 1982 grew at least sevenfold, from 600 to 4,300, and probably more. And somehow people have the idea there's something wrong about this. Some of them are simply offended by the undignified spectacle of all these reporters and minicams and photographers trailing after the president and shouting and jostling for position. And with some, I think, even if they don't articulate it, there's a feeling of "This is too big." It's always that way, of course—power and bigness alarm people and frighten people.

But there's a double standard at work here with respect to the press. I don't want to get paranoid. I've seen too many paranoid politicians. But nevertheless a double standard is being applied to the press, because elsewhere in the American society bigness is considered very, very good. It's considered a desirable thing. We used to have literally scores of automobile companies; now we have three. The entire trend of the American economy has been toward bigness.

Bigness works and smallness is inefficient. Well, when the same thing happens with the news media, which are themselves big business, free enterprise—somehow something is wrong with it.

Now, I'm going to give you a little comment, if I may, on something that Helen said at the beginning of her very admirable presentation. She made a reference to the famous Herblock cartoon in early 1969, after Nixon had been inaugurated. Herblock, as Helen points out, had always pictured Nixon with a villanous five o'clock shadow. But now he drew a cartoon showing himself as a barber and offering Nixon a free shave, in other words, a fresh start. OK, the reporters remembered the McCarthy era, we remembered Jerry Voorhis, we remembered Helen Gahagan Douglas, we remembered the '62 gubernatorial election in California where they set up this phony Democrats-for-Nixon committee, using people's names without their permission or without even notifying them. Pat Brown took them to court, it was so flagrant. So we remembered all the demagoguery and all the dirty tricks, because the dirty tricks were operating even that early. There was nothing new about Watergate. As Victor Lasky said, it had happened before. Yes, it had happened before—under Nixon.

All right. We remembered all that, but what Herblock was doing was symbolizing the attitude that prevailed in the press corps. Nixon was now President of the United States, and as Lyndon Johnson said we only have one president at a time. If he succeeds, we succeed. If he fails, we fail. So there was going to be a honeymoon. The press was offering this man a honeymoon. That's what the Herblock cartoon symbolized. They were offering a fresh start in their relationship with him.

Now I want to give you Nixon's reaction, because it is not generally known what his reaction was. Jim Keogh, who was his speechwriter, attended Nixon's first cabinet meeting before the Inauguration. It took place on December 12, 1968. Nixon had been supported by 80 percent of America's newspapers, so the honeymoon spirit was in the air, and here was Nixon's reaction, as reported by Keogh:

> Always remember that the men and women of the news media approach this as an adversary relationship. The time will come when they will run lies about you. And the columnists and editorial writers will make you seem to be scoundrels or fools or both. And the cartoonists will depict you as ogres. Some of your wives will get up in the morning and look at the papers and start to cry. Now, don't let this get you down, don't let it defeat you and don't try to adjust your actions to what you think will please

them. Do what you think is the right thing to do and let the criticism roll off your back. Don't think that the criticism you see or hear in one or two places is all that is getting through to the public.

It's that first sentence I want to draw to your attention. "Always remember the men and the women of the news media approach this as an adversary relationship." In other words, it didn't make any difference whether the press was offering this man a honeymoon or not. As far as he was concerned, there could not be a honeymoon. He wasn't going to have a honeymoon because he was absolutely convinced that the press was implacably opposed to him.

MS. THOMAS: And he had felt that way since 1940.

MR. DEAKIN: He had felt that way ever since he had discovered that the *Los Angeles Times* was not the only newspaper in America. As long as all he had to read was the *Los Angeles Times*, which was coddling him and giving no space to his opponents and playing him up as the great, young anti-Communist Congressman and so forth, he thought that's all the press was. Then all of a sudden he discovered there were other papers besides the *Times*.

MS. THOMAS: I think that the public reaction is understandable. They see us shouting at the president, in terms of the quicky so-called ten minute press conferences. It's very competitive, we're each shouting to get a question in, and the TV people are even more competitive because they have their cameras there and they have to make good for their bosses as well as imagewise. It's a real scramble, and ten minutes is certainly not enough to develop anything before Speakes panics and cuts it off. This is what they consider a feeding, and knowing that this would come across like a bunch of banshees to the public. We all get mail: How can you treat the president like this, you horrible person, and so forth. They'll never understand.

Also I think I resent quite a bit the columnists who do sit in their ivory towers after we scramble for one word from a president and I mean one. They can sit can back and say: the president said this today. One day the president was walking out of the White House and I said, "Mr. President, is there a recession on?" As he stepped into his helicopter he said, "Yes." This is the kind of thing. Weeks could go by when you wouldn't have a press conference to ever ask him that. But you are there, you're there in the middle of the night, you're there at five o'clock in the morning or whatever time it's necessary to get one assessment.

MR. DEAKIN: I've got to tell you a story about Lyndon Johnson to add to that list. Helen is one of these reporters who lives for the honest answer that you occasionally get. During the Dominican crisis—you remember this, Helen—this was when twenty-five hundred people allegedly had their heads chopped off, the whole business. During the Dominican crisis, Johnson had this incredible walking press conference when he talked about our people being killed and the U.S. Ambassador telephoning from under his desk while the bullets were whistling by. And all of this was just absolutely untrue. Furthermore, two weeks had gone by and there had been plenty of time to check and Johnson was still giving out wrong information and declassifying secret reports from the CIA on the spot. That didn't seem to work. Sending the Marines to the Dominican Republic wasn't selling. So he came up with a new justification for it, and it was the standard justification—the Commies are behind it. The Dominican revolution is about to go Communist.

MS. THOMAS: First explanation for it was to protect the Americans.

MR. DEAKIN: Yes, first it was to protect the Americans. That didn't work. So then he switched to the Commie threat in the Dominican Republic. He started saying the revolt had been taken over by the Communists. He doled out that line, the national security line. And then he held another walking press conference. John Chancellor was covering for NBC at that time, and John, not anticipating the kind of answer he was going to get, said, "Mr. President, at what point did you discover that the Dominican revolution was being taken over by the Communists?" He stopped and said, "At no time." It was the only time he told the truth in the whole crisis.

MR. CORMIER: I'd like to raise a point. I think that a lot of what Helen has been talking about is the necessity for the press to corner the president wherever they can, sometimes in a fashion that is a little unseemly, maybe. This really points back to a fundamental failure by Reagan to implement as promised the recommendations of the Miller Center Commission on presidential press conferences with respect to the frequency of holding these conferences.

If the man were available, as the Commission suggested and as he should be, this all would become quite unnecessary.

MR. DEAKIN: They may be sitting down for the press conference,

Ken, in response to your report. But the other thing you called for was frequency of press conferences.

MR. JONES: In those statements the two characterizations that comes through to me most—both fascinating statements and descriptions of the relationship—are skepticism and cynicism, above all. Are these characteristics essential for doing a good job?

MR. DEAKIN: Yes on number one. If a reporter isn't skeptical of official statements, he is not a reporter. If a reporter is not skeptical of what not just the government but everyone tells him, what is the impetus for him to go on and try to find out what the truth is? If he just accepts it—oh, you say that black is white, all right I'll put it in my paper that black is white—what kind of reporting is that? Is that journalism? Is that communication, maintaining a conduit of information? Skepticism is absolutely vital.

Now cynicism depends. I spent twenty-five years covering the White House, and after it reached a certain point I had to guard against paralytic cynicism. Because I had seen so much human folly, so many mistakes, so many lies, that I had to pull myself up short all the time and say: yes, I understand. They are human beings, they are under pressure, they are lying because they wish to prevail, they want their policies and programs to prevail. I must understand why they are lying. I must not permit myself to become paralytically cynical, to the point that I cannot ever see a good motive or worthwhile motive in anything. I have to guard against that.

MR. THOMAS: I can see ourselves as believers. We have enough for a book on them in terms of skepticism, but we still are believers. Every day we go to the White House we expect to get the truth, we work to get the truth, and we put out what we can get.

MR. DEAKIN: You know what reporters at the White House are, or reporters covering·city hall or the governor or anybody else? They're just like the American people in one respect. They all live by Dr. Johnson's dictum. Dr. Johnson said, "Mankind lives from hope to hope." The last hope is always disappointed but you live for that next one.

MS. THOMAS: I don't think you see cynics in the press corps.

MR. DEAKIN: Every time the president goes on television and makes *his* pitch and defends *his* programs, he has access to the American people to make his case, in that one-way communication we were talking about. And every time that happens, the press is saying implicitly: OK, we'll give you the benefit of the doubt. Tell us. We give you the facility, we give you time on the air waves, we give you the space in the newspaper, every time we print that State of the

Union message, that budget message, that economic report—in all of it, we're saying we're giving you the benefit of the doubt. Tell us what you plan to do; tell us your reasons for it. We are not saying to you, no, no, we don't believe it from the beginning so we won't print it and we won't put it on TV.

I mean, what are we talking about here folks? There's one hell of a lot of cooperation and help, sheer help for the president from the press. We're not out there destroying this guy from the moment he gets in. We're giving him that time on TV to make his case. He may raise hell about the instant analysis that comes afterward. In the days when they were really attacking instant analysis, during the Nixon administration, people were saying, how come they let David Brinkley and Eric Sevareid and the other pundits come on right after the president and pick everything he says to pieces? It's a liberal conspiracy to destroy this man, to destroy the president, conveniently ignoring the fact that the president had just spent half an hour on national television making *his* case.

MS. THOMAS: And sometimes the analysis isn't picking it apart; it's simply saying, to sum up, this is what he's saying and what they'll do and so forth.

MR. JONES: Does the scepticism drive the determination of truth? In any one event there are a number of truths depending on how people see it.

MS. THOMAS: Neither Jim Deakin nor I really touched on the fact that there obviously is a handbook of cliché answers handed down from one press secretary to another to avoid telling you anything, to avoid telling you the truth sometimes but to avoid maybe outright lying: "I have no knowledge of that," "I'm not aware of that," etc. Then Larry Speakes has developed this. If you ask what you think is a telling question because he put something on the table—now, about the budget and so forth, Speakes came out and said we've narrowed the differences. He took the line that Baker had given him. Well, they had not narrowed the differences at all. And then when you challenge him the next day it goes on. On Friday when the unemployment figures came out, ten million unemployed, and so forth he stated the Reagan line because it's all the Democrats' fault. I claim that it's George Washington's fault.

MR. DEAKIN: Yes, because you can work every one of these all the way back.

MS. THOMAS: And so it was the Democrats' fault and so forth and Reagan has always said when the ten percent cut comes in on July 1 that's when his program will work. To Speakes I said, "Now you say that the Democrats are at fault but you are predicting an up-turn now. My question is, when does Reagan take responsibility for the economy, for the country, for whatever is happening? Can he say on July 1 that this is the date, this is the deadline?" He refused to answer. If you knew the frustration. Skepticism, we don't even have enough skepticism. You are constantly being defied on simple questions.

MR. DEAKIN: You know Lady Bird had to ask the Secret Service whether Lyndon Johnson was going to Texas. If you think we have trouble getting information—his own wife.

MR. CORMIER: On the question of scepticism versus possible truth, it seems to me that it is a truism that when the White House or the president says something it's much the same as Joe McCarthy the first time waving the list of alleged Communists. If what he says is wrong, it takes time for the press to catch up with the fact that he's wrong. His story is reported, more often than not, undiluted, first crack out of the box. Then reporters are skeptical, they start wondering, then you may get the follow-up stories that say, well maybe it isn't quite that way.

MS. THOMAS: That's the story of the disability, the man in the Virginia area. Reagan gave an interview for the *Oklahoma Daily,* they were very, very sympathetic. They said "You're right, Mr. President." He brought up that he's always being accused that these cuts in benefits are hurting people, he brought up this man who applied for disability, was offered a job and he wouldn't work, and how the government was really being taken. Well, his story stayed for a day or two. Then a few of us began to check into this question, the man was being interviewed, and he was sort of arbitrarily taken off of disability. The story is not unique. But they proceeded to show that this was—actually the cuts had come about through the Carter administration. They failed to say that Reagan had accelerated the program where there would be less inspection of anyone's right to have disability or not.

And then they read the social security regulations which will astound you. It seems that this man was a worker, a welder, and he had been hit on the head so he suffered from seizures and became progressively bad. The Social Security regulation said that he did not have enough seizures to merit payments! Then you say how many seizures does he have to have? Anyway, Frank's point is right, that the president can say something and then it takes you three days, if you have a reporter who wanted to follow it up, to see if it is true.

MR. DEAKIN: Only in recent years have people in Nevada and Utah, particularly Utah, begun filing suits against the government over atomic tests that the government said at the time were harmless.

One-way communication, the government's version, the government's statement, the government's version of the truth. The press in this case didn't exercise skepticism. It accepted the official version. Now thirty years later we find that the leukemia rate among children in those Utah communities is scores of times higher than the national average, and people are dying off like flies. They're dying at forty instead of living to seventy. Only now, thirty years too late, are some reporters beginning to exercise skepticism, and even then it was only when the suits began to be filed. Often we can't find out. But if the skepticism wasn't there we would *never* find out.

MR. CORMIER: The hope is in the skepticism.

MR. YOUNG: I've read two articles recently, one by Tony Lewis and one by somebody, I forget who, out of the *New York Times* who was reporting on the Congress, on the mood of the Congress. And I would just like to have your comments about this in the context of your discussion. One of the points that Tony Lewis made in his article, it was on reportage, was about Reagan. You're undoubtedly familiar with it and I think I remember that one of the points he made was that, he was asking why the press was being so kind to Reagan when they know the truth about his state of mind, about his ability, and so on. It was rather striking and I didn't know quite what to make of it. It may have something to do with the honeymoon, maybe he's all off base—I would just like your comments about it.

The other thing I want to ask you about, the article on Congress, was a betrayal of the mood and mind-set of a certain group of new-breed congressmen, and one of them was quoted as saying, or words to this effect, that the President lies.

MS. THOMAS: Who says that?

MR. YOUNG: One of the congressmen quoted. And I wonder if that mood, if you'd encountered it. What do you do with that as a reporter?

MR. DEAKIN: If you say something in the newspaper or on television, and you can't document it, your editor will take that statement out, if he's on the ball. I get asked all the time, why didn't the press print anything about John F. Kennedy's sex life, the fact that he was chasing women all the time? How, since this always comes from the far right, I always answer: For the same reason we didn't print anything about Nixon's drinking. But the fact is if we couldn't document it we couldn't print it.

MR. YOUNG: I was struck by the fact that it was a reporter writing this statement.

MR. DEAKIN: Tony Lewis is very liberal. But Tony Lewis in this instance was forgetting the fact that if you can't document something, you can't print it. Look at the trouble the *Washington Post* got in when it printed something that its editors had let get by without demanding that the reporter document it; demanding to know who's your source when you say you've discovered this eight-year-old heroin addict named Jimmy. They didn't do it. They got themselves in terrible trouble.

MS. THOMAS: We don't write our personal opinions. Tony is absolutely wrong. His only perceptions of Reagan come through us. He's never there. He doesn't man the barricade. Far from it. He's off in the Middle East or somewhere else. What he knows about the President we have told him. And we have told him as factually as possible.

I believe in objective reporting. I believe there is certainly a place for it, and there's certainly a place for Tony. I love his writing, but I think he's absolutely wrong. In those euphoric moments after presidents become presidents, we may say, let him get his feet wet; but the question of judging him every day—we lay it down: this president has said this. And other reporters take off from there and see if it's so or not. But, "He said, he added," is still first.

MR. CORMIER: Let me get in something here. I know of only one instance where the White House press corps has semi-grappled with something that we did not want to write about on a president's trip. And that was when Jerry Ford was first in office. It sometimes seemed to us that he took a martini or two too many and we wondered how do we deal with this? Well, he went up to Boston and made a speech and *Newsweek*—I must say it was the only publication with the guts to do it—simply made an offhand reference to him slurring his words when he spoke. I never saw Jerry Ford approaching insobriety again.

MR. THOMPSON: You did draw a number of examples from foreign policy? Does that mean—maybe this is a "When did you stop beating your wife?" type question—that you would have doubts about the distinction between foreign policy matters and domestic policy matters? It is often argued that there are some issues where you, the reporter, can't expect to get to the heart of the issue when serious business is going on? It concerned Camp David, and presumably it concerns some of the negotiations going on now? Are there some constraints on what the reporters can find out, necessarily, about foreign policy, given its nature? Should there be a possibility for an administration, when highly sensitive issues and negotiations are in a make or break stage, to get away from reporters and get away from publicity?

MS. THOMAS: I believe in an almost total open society. I believe that we should know as much as possible about foreign policy, particularly when the President himself says you have seventeen minutes to get out of town before the bomb falls. I think the people should be alert as to what's happening. I think too much is suppressed. I would want no blocks in the legitimacy of the pursuit of trying to find out what they're doing in the foreign policy field. Perhaps there are some very legitimate military secrets and I don't think we ever really try to pull those. We try to find out what's going on. So much was suppressed and there was so much deception in Vietnam, for example. Those kind of things. The President has an NSC meeting, national security council meeting, maybe once a week, sometimes more. He will never say it's an emergency meeting and will never give you the topic. And once in a while you'll want to leak it, as three newspapers, for example, had on Thursday I think it was, that Reagan would propose a fifty-fifty equal deterrent and so forth. The story obviously came from the same source and had been placed with about three papers. My feeling is that we should try to find out as much as possible and that certainly foreign policy and national security should not be off-limits. I don't understand why the Americans will be hurt if they find out what's going on.

MR. DEAKIN: Well, skepticism as far as journalists are concerned, is based on experience. You know, there's a collective memory that journalists have when they have been in Washington for a long time, a greater memory of what's happened before than some people who are coming in for the first time to run the government, people who've never been in Washington before, which is usually the case with each new administration. So, reporters have a collective memory of these things that administrations usually don't have, unless they bring in a lot of old hands. And the collective memory that the journalists have is of time after time after time, instance after instance after instance, in which the government claimed that the security of the nation would be impaired or endangered if certain information were made public. Then the information was made public, did get into the press, and *nothing happened.* There was never the slightest evidence that it was of any aid to any adversary or enemy of the United States. Nobody took advantage of us in some negotiations or threatened us with any kind of military or nuclear blackmail. In other words, all the dangers that the government said would happen if certain information were made public did not materialize. They all turned out to be chimeras. So we get very skeptical about this claim of national security.

The classic instance, and I'm going to give you several, was the

Pentagon Papers. The *New York Times* had obtained the Pentagon Papers. The Nixon administration wasn't even involved in the Pentagon Papers; they didn't cover the Nixon administration. Nevertheless, after an initial period of trying to figure out what to do, they went to court and got an injunction against the *New York Times* and subsequently other newspapers on the grounds that the publication of the Pentagon Papers would endanger the national security. It went all the way to the Supreme Court and it was very narrowly held that the *New York Times* and the other papers had the right to publish the Pentagon Papers. And so the rest of the Pentagon Papers came out and all this danger to national security didn't materialize. It wasn't there.

Let me give you two or three other examples. After Johnson left the presidency he was interviewed by Walter Cronkite. And Cronkite asked Johnson whether his last secretary of defense, Clark Clifford, had been responsible for the bombing pause in Vietnam. I don't know Johnson's motives, but apparently he didn't want Clifford to get the credit for having advocated and persuaded Johnson to stop the bombing of North Vietnam. So in an effort to show that it was not Clifford who had done this, Johnson pulled a document out of his pocket—and this was before a national television audience—and he read this paper which showed that on such and such a date he, Johnson, had ordered the study of possible alternatives to the bombing. And Johnson announced—he didn't imply it, he stated it explicitly—that this was a classified document, a national security document. And he wasn't even president at the time; he was a former president. He simply declassified this document on national television and read it to the American people. He did this constantly in press conferences, especially the press conferences he had on the lawn. He would pull out something and it was classified, a CIA report or a Pentagon report, and because it served his purpose to give out the information he declassified it on the spot. Other presidents have done similar things many times—leaking national security information. The Reagan administration has done it whenever it suited their purpose.

Now, the question that arises is this: If the information was such that it imperiled or might imperil the security of the United States, but the next moment it was no threat to the American people so it could be declassified, then what are we supposed to say national security is? And what we come down to, unfortunately, is that national security consists of what the president says it is at any given moment. But that is a very relative kind of definition. It's not a very absolute kind of definition. It's not something you can rely on very much.

MS. THOMAS: And it's also so that the people will not get in on the dialogue. They will not be able to say anything. It is a *fait accompli,* any time they want to make a decision, nobody else is able to get in on it and decide whether it's right or wrong.

MR. DEAKIN: Or if they do get in on it they only get in on the government's terms. It declassifies the information and gives it out. One-way communication. Let me give you another example. Johnson held a summit meeting with Premier Kosygin in Glassboro, New Jersey. It was all secret. The reporters weren't told anything. All we got was, you know, the length of the meeting. We weren't told what they talked about, what the results were or anything else because, of course, that would affect national security; that was a national security matter. So as soon as it was over Johnson flew to Texas and he invited Max Frankel, who was then covering the White House for the *New York Times,* out to the ranch. They take a swim together and Johnson is standing in the water and proceeds to give Frankel a one-hour report on everything that was discussed at the summit meeting. And Frankel is free to use it. So what is this national security stuff?

Here is another example. George Christian, who was Johnson's press secretary for the last two years, attended the so-called troika meeting that Johnson held every Friday morning with McNamara and Rostow, in which they made Vietnam policy. He was there every Friday for two years. But we never could get one word out of Christian about what was said in those meetings until they were ready to announce something. If they had something to announce, they announced it. But we could never find out what the pros and cons were, what considerations they were weighing, what their thinking was, what they were doing. Not a word—couldn't get a word out of them for two solid years. Then Johnson leaves office and Christian writes a book. And Max Frankel talks about this book in his deposition in the Pentagon Papers case, and Frankel says there are seventy pages of that book that contain classified information. We couldn't be given it at the time, the American people couldn't be given it, but he could put it in a book.

MR. THOMPSON: Do you think there would have been a Camp David agreement if reporters had been allowed to mingle with the negotiators?

MS. THOMAS: Of course. It was just a question of Carter twisting Begin's arm off. We all knew it was going on. I don't understand why it had to be so secret. We were never allowed to even send one photographer there in—how long was it? More than a week. No, I don't see why all this had to be in total secrecy.

MR. DEAKIN: The American people have to pay for these decisions. They've got to pay for them, either in money or blood or loss of affluence or whatever it may be. They've got to pay for it. But they're not going to be told about it until, as Helen says, it is a *fait accompli.*

MS. THOMAS: Why should it be twenty-five years later in a White Paper. What good's that?

MR. THOMPSON: If my wife and I have any difficulties we have to work it out and the best chance for working it out is in private.

MS. THOMAS: Yes, but you don't control millions of people and their fates.

MR. THOMPSON: Well, the method is the same and we've learned that the open covenants openly arrived at works if the open arrived part isn't emphasized too much.

MS. THOMAS: I don't agree at all.

MR. CORMIER: I would throw in one thing here. Without defending the secrecy there, we were suddenly in a position of dealing with substance in the form of rumors that were appearing in the Israeli and the Arabian press. And oftentimes they were very well informed, much better informed than we were. We were getting it from the Middle East reporters. We knew nothing.

MR. DEAKIN: Do you know that practically every president we've had has been far more candid and far more frank and far more open with the foreign press than he is with the American press? Almost every one of them. They will talk to Henry Brandon and the British journalists and the French journalists and tell them things they'll never tell us. It's safe for the British and French to read about it, but it's not safe for the American people.

MS. THOMAS: In the bombing of Cambodia, for fourteen months the Cambodians knew they were being bombed, the Vietnamese knew that bombing was going on, the Russians knew the bombing was going on, the Chinese knew the bombing was going on. So why the secrecy? The secrecy was simply not to scare hell out of the American people and say that Nixon is widening this war while all the time he's saying he's pulling out.

MR. THOMPSON: What would you have said in the papers if you had known—maybe you did—that Hamilton Jordan was sitting up with the Panamanian head of state all hours of the night trying to get the last pieces of the Panama treaty worked out?

MS. THOMAS: Fine. What's wrong with that?

MR. DEAKIN: You think if we had said it, that would have stopped them from doing it? If they really wanted to do it?

MS. THOMAS: What's wrong with that?

MR. THOMPSON: First thing you would have said was that he didn't have any experience and that would have gotten flashed around the world. The second thing—

MS. THOMAS: Everybody knew he didn't have experience. Torrijos knew he didn't have any experience. I mean he came right out of Georgia and had no foreign policy background.

MR. THOMPSON: But they finally worked out the last—

MS. THOMAS: He was acting under Carter's orders. He was an emissary at the time.

MR. DEAKIN: The mere fact that the press says somebody is doing something has no legal force to prevent people from going right on and doing something. If they do stop, it's usually because they are doing something wrong.

MS. THOMAS: When this administration started making sounds like a little war in El Salvador might possibly occur, it gave the impression that they rule out nothing so they could send troops there. The administration, the White House was bombarded with letters from parents saying hell no, we won't go. They sent all these letters over to the State Department, I mean, the White House was not going to get this.

MR. THOMPSON: You would acknowledge there are some appropriate areas of quiet diplomacy?

MS. THOMAS: No. I like to know as much as possible and to be able to transmit as much as possible.

MR. DEAKIN: It depends on so many things. I think it's impossible to speak for the American press; it is not monolithic. We have conservative publications and liberal publications, conservative reporters and liberal reporters—you can't generalize. I suspect that if there was more candor from the administration about the factors that go into making decisions in foreign policy and so forth, national security matters, that it would ease some of the pressure and would actually permit them to do more of the quiet diplomacy. Because nothing disarms a reporter so much as feeling that he or she is being given some information. That's what they live for; that's what they exist for. Give them some information and go right back behind closed doors. It takes some of the heat off, and you can go on and do more of your quiet diplomacy without the press breathing down your neck. Because you're giving them something; you're giving them something to put in the paper or on the tube. I'm not saying that that is going to stop them. I'm not saying that they're not going to continue to go at you hammer and tongs for more; they'll always ask for more. So it's just a speculation on my part, that if they were more candid about things, and really, they could be candid about things without doing any real danger, they probably would take some of the heat off themselves. It is a matter of human nature. If you are absolutely told no, you can't do something, that increases your interest in doing it. And if reporters are told no, we won't tell you anything, they get that much more energetic in trying to find out something. But if they're given a little something, it takes the heat off. The analogy is with Bismarck. Otto was no liberal, but what he did with the Social Democratic party in Germany was to throw them a little bone here, a little bone there, a little bit of social welfare. Milk for nursing mothers. And what happened was that it quieted the Social Democrats in the Bundestag. It toned them down because he gave them a little something. If you do this with reporters, you'll get pretty much the same result.

MR. CORMIER: We're easily manipulated.

MR. JONES: In this national security area, I wonder if there are some limits. I watched the marvelous program on Oppenheimer. Is that a case, the development of a weapon during the kind of war that World War II was, is that a case where the press should not report, that we should insist on secrecy?

MS. THOMAS: I think it would have been much safer for the Japanese to know, that might have stopped a lot of killing.

MR. DEAKIN: The reason for it was because it was wartime and there was a censorship program. It was a voluntary censorship program that the press adhered to almost completely. There was the exception of the *Chicago Tribune* with the Japanese Purple Code. Otherwise this massive institution, the American press, adhered to the voluntary censorship program with practically one hundred percent compliance and the secret Manhattan project was kept secret throughout the entire war.

MR. CORMIER: But not by us. It was kept by the government.

MR. DEAKIN: Well, they also did a very good job of keeping the secret.

MS. THOMAS: Well, my point is maybe if it had been publicized that such a bomb existed finally and the U.S. was ready to use it maybe the Japanese could have saved themselves.

MR. DEAKIN: There's a problem with that, Helen, because if that had happened and it had got back to Hitler then we might have pushed Hitler into developing the atomic bomb.

MR. CORMIER: There is a sense of limits. I'm not quite sure what it is.

MR. DEAKIN: There have to be limits. But if the press is asked to exercise sound judgment and agree to limits, especially in wartime, then the government has to understand that there are limits on the limitation of information. Instead, we've come to the point now where everything is classified.

MR. JONES: Oftentimes one comes away from something like that Oppenheimer program with all of us saying that maybe there should have been more consideration—

MS. THOMAS: My feeling is that I have found out that any time a big secret has been revealed it has been more helpful to world knowledge and more important than the harm it does.

MR. BLACKFORD: Back in 1956 the CIA got Khrushchev's speech. And we still don't know how they got it. Does it make any difference?

MS. THOMAS: Out of Warsaw, huh?

MR. BLACKFORD: Does it make any difference how they got it out? The news is the speech, is it not?

MS. THOMAS: That's right. It's interesting in a replay of how it did happen but that wouldn't be the big part. The speech was the important thing and it really shocked the world.

MR. DEAKIN: But you can turn that one around and you can say ah, hah! Isn't that an obvious example where national security should have been maintained? Shouldn't that have been a closely held secret? We shouldn't have let the Russians know that we had that kind of intelligence, expertise, and facilities. But no, as soon as it suits the government's purpose to have it out, it comes out—and that's the point about national security. National security ceases to exist the moment the government decides that the information will be of some assistance to it.

We've seen this now with Reagan over and over and over again. Stuff that was absolutely secret classified information is suddenly released. Weinberger did it with the Soviet capability assessment. One moment something is top secret. The next moment they can use it, so they put it out.

MS. THOMAS: They flipped out when there was a report that we were helping the British [in the Falklands] with intelligence. They really flipped out. All kinds of running around finding the leakers and stuff. I think that most Americans would assume we are helping the British with intelligence. So I don't understand those kinds of mentality.

CO-OPTION OF THE PRESS

Frank Cormier

MR. THOMPSON: Let's move on to the presentation by Frank Cormier. Frank Cormier was born in Worcester, Massachusetts. He served for eighteen years covering the White House, was successor to Merriman Smith as senior White House correspondent. He is the author of five books, a sixth in press and a seventh in his head or partly finished. Frank was a participant in the preliminary stages of our press conference commission. I won't take any more time but we're delighted you're with us.

MR. CORMIER: Thank you, Ken. John Kennedy has been quoted as saying that presidents must form their friendships before they reach the White House because it won't be practical afterwards. Presidents do form friendships, of course, and so do we reporters. All of us are living flesh and, except for the aberrant, all of us, and most especially presidents, prefer having friends to enemies. But the problems arise when presidents and reporters become friendly with each other—something that you might not have considered in the discussion here so far today. Problems of this sort are found in all facets of journalism. Reporters inevitably want to get close to their sources because tips and leaks from friendly sources can add to our reporting and they do us no harm with our bosses.

By the same token, sources, whether they be presidents or city managers or whatever, know the benefit of cultivating friendships with reporters. And understandably they want their versions of controversial events to be printed or broadcast. Equally important, reporters are apt to mute, if not avoid, material that is critical of friendly sources. It happens and we all know it does. The perils of the situation are obvious. Yet we read little about this except when a

60

woman reporter in Philadelphia is exposed as the mistress of a shadowy politician, or when a Pulitzer Prize winning male reporter openly writes speeches for a Republican presidential candidate. I suspect that a good number of us here have heard rumors that one nationally known woman reporter was bedded by two presidents, Kennedy and Johnson. If true, she certainly set some kind of indoor olympic record. I don't know if the rumors are true or not. But they certainly are not implausible at all, which should tell us something about the situation. Reporters and sources belly up to each other in ways that almost defy credulity. Earl Mazo once told me that when he was political writer for the old *New York Herald Tribune* Lyndon Johnson had offered him the sexual favors of an attractive Johnson secretary. All Mazo had to do in return was cover LBJ's southern whistle stop tour in 1960. Alas, no one knows whether Johnson was really serious about this because Earl declined to make the trip.

Stories like these are fodder for press room bull sessions. But rarely do you read such things in print. In the case of friendships between presidents and reporters I know of only one book that deals with the benefits and perils involved. The book is *Conversations with Kennedy* by Ben Bradlee. He was a political reporter for *Newsweek's* Washington bureau when he met John Kennedy. But Bradlee's book deals only superficially with the topic of friendship at the summit of our national life. Wrote Bradlee, "It happens to very few of us that some neighbor, some family friend, someone whose children play with your children becomes President of the United States. It now seems clear that when it happened to me that friendship dominated my life, as Walter Lippmann had warned me it could." Well, Bradlee's offhand reference to Lippmann's warning was followed immediately by a recitation of the benefits he derived from the friendship: "It was invaluable to me as a journalist and I used it without embarrassment to give *Newsweek* the intimate details of the life and thinking of this remarkable man."

Kennedy, Bradlee and their wives became friends in 1959, just as Senator Kennedy began his campaign for the presidency. It was, of course, a campaign that Bradlee covered. And the friendship was followed by Bradlee's promotion to Washington bureau chief of the magazine, an elevation that may not have been coincidental. Clearly, Bradlee gained much from the friendship that dominated his life, by his own account. And Kennedy gained a sympathetic reportorial ear. The readers of *Newsweek* gained exclusive insights into the personality and promises of a successful candidate and a popular president. So who was the loser? We can't really be sure there was a loser. Bradlee himself seems reasonably satisfied that everyone emerged a winner. As he said in his book, "I never wrote less that I knew about him, filing the good with the bad, but obviously the information that Kennedy gave me tended to put him and his policies in a favorable light."

One must wonder if at least some of Bradlee's reporting might have turned out differently if he and Kennedy had approached each other at arm's length. Bradlee surely was aware of the potential pitfalls, and seems to have been at least vaguely troubled by them. At one point in *Conversations with Kennedy* he acknowledged, "This thing I had going with the junior Senator from Massachusetts was very seductive," and on the same page there seems to me to be almost a plaintive element in another striking affirmation by Bradlee, "If I was had, so be it. I doubt I will ever be so close to a political figure again."

Now, I believe every reporter in this room could make a similar statement about a close and friendly source, president or otherwise. I could say it about Lyndon Johnson, adding two amendments. With the benefit of hindsight, I know I was had more than once, but I insist that my up and down relationship with Johnson, which involved several hundred hours of palaver, in which my colleagues here often shared, stopped well short of intimate friendship. I believe Helen Thomas and Jim Deakin were in much the same boat. So, here in this room we have three reporters who have had frequent dealings with presidents, at varying levels of intimacy, but intimacy nonetheless. Three out of three is a pretty good batting average. It underscores my point that dealings between presidents and reporters spawn problems that are too frequent to be ignored.

Kennedy's friendships with the press, perhaps without exception, predated his presidency, but very few predated his campaign for the presidency. Leaving aside Ben Bradlee and Charley Bartlett, consider Kennedy's friendships with Sandy Vanocur, Hugh Sidey, Bill Lawrence, and a lot of others. I doubt that any of these relationships would have flourished except in a campaign environment. In that setting they are unquestionably mutually beneficial. And the benefits carried over into Kennedy's presidency.

I cannot argue that there is something inherently wrong about these relationships, any more than I would suggest that Helen should have spurned the friendship of Martha Mitchell. But I do say that such ties are potentially hazardous to impartial reporting. As journalists, we must guard against being had and we should take a particularly critical look at everything we write, especially the things we write about sources we like or admire. That we will like or admire some more than others is inevitable. We are human beings and citizens, no matter how apolitical we strive to be.

In thirty years in the business I've known only one reporter who flatly refused to talk to any president lest he be influenced. That was the late James Marlow who wrote a column five days a week for the Associated Press. In a sense, Marlow and I turned out to occupy flip sides of the same coin. In 1964, I must confess, I admired Lyndon Johnson extravangantly. On civil rights I thought he was the greatest leader since Lincoln. And I still feel that way. My admiration was such that I'd tried to convert Marlow, who looked at LBJ with a very jaundiced eye and even questioned the President's sanity. Then came 1965. Suddenly I had to balance the triumph of the Voting Rights Act against Johnson's involvement in Vietnam. My admiration for the President fell rather precipitously. But Marlow was an old cold war warrior. He believed passionately in the domino theory. Abruptly, he was telling me that the President was a great man. Before long Marlow abandoned his reluctance to talk to presidents. He began visiting Johnson at the White House, sometimes late at night. He even began offering advice: Dwight Eisenhower was in Walter Reed Hospital and Marlow urged Johnson to go see him. Johnson not only went and saw him but he took Marlow along for the ride.

Such are the seductions of proximity to power. And because Jim Marlow succumbed, as did Walter Lippmann for a time, I suspect no one is totally immune. In these circumstances we must try very hard to keep our personal gyroscopes in working order, and it isn't always easy.

I'm ashamed, really, to think how far out of line I got one night in 1964. During a long flight on Air Force One Johnson conceded he would beat Barry Goldwater handily. He said he was campaigning hard because he wanted deserving Democrats to grab his coattails. And then he asked the four reporters present for the names of the congressional Republicans they felt were most worthy of defeat. He promised that either he or Hubert Humphrey would campaign against them. It was an incredible proposition but two of us regretably succumbed. More accurately, we permitted ourselves to be seduced, to surrender our political independence. One of my colleagues, who soon became a well-known Washington bureau chief, urged Johnson to campaign against a rising but still rather obscure House member from Kansas named Robert Dole. Two days later, true to his word, Johnson changed his campaign itinerary to go into Dole's district. For my part, I told the President I had been voting for ten years against a very conservative northern Virginia Republican, Joel Broyhill.

Johnson promptly announced he would hold two rallies in Broyhill's district.

It's so easy to go along with presidents even in unthinkable situations. Particularly striking was an encounter five of us had with LBJ just six weeks after he took office. We were flying back to Washington from Texas on Air Force One. The late Merriman Smith was in the press pool with me along with two others when Johnson suddenly appeared at our table with a personal guest, Scotty Reston. I gave up my seat to the President and squatted in the aisle with Reston. At that time, you will recall, as Jim has alluded to earlier, Johnson was telling everyone, "I need your help." Citing the emergency created by Kennedy's assassination, he tried to make deals with everyone, the press included. Peering intently at us, LBJ declared, "I'll tell you everything. You'll be as well informed as any member of the cabinet. There won't be any secrets except for where the national security is involved. Of course, I may go into a strange bedroom every now and then that I won't want you to write about, but otherwise you can write everything." Well, he was offering us pie in the sky and he was off the record to boot. But this was only the beginning. There was a quid pro quo, to which Jim has also already alluded:

> I need your help. If I succeed, then you succeed. We all succeed or fall together. With your help I'll do the best job that's in me for our country. I don't want Jack Kennedy looking down at me from heaven saying he picked the wrong vice president. But I can't do the job alone. I need your help. There's no reason why the members of the White House press corps shouldn't be the best informed, most respected, highest paid reporters in Washington. If you help me, I'll help you and make you all big men in your profession.

Well, it was a strange statement to make. Reston and Smitty, they already had everything they wanted. Moreover, I thought it was a shocking statement. In the silence that followed I waited for my elders and betters to say something. But their continued silence underscored the fact that Americans are reluctant to challenge their president. So finally I said something. "Mr. President," I said, "don't you know that sooner or later every reporter around this table is going to write something that will make you mad as hell?" Well, he stared at me in disbelief. "I have never gotten mad at a newsman in my life," he said, "except for one NBC man and he broke my confidence." And then he invoked the name of Jack Bell, who was AP's political writer at the time and something of a legend. Pounding on the table, Johnson started shouting at me, "I don't even get mad at Jack Bell and he writes black Republican stories."

Every president, I'm convinced, does his best to co-op the press or, at the very least, to keep us docile and friendly. Jack Kennedy was better at it than anyone I've met. And LBJ worked harder at it, with limited success, than anyone I've known. Never before, or since, has any president had so many journalists as weekend guests in his home. Scotty Reston, Merriman Smith, Hugh Sidey, Ray Scherer, Bill Gill, Tom Wicker, Bill Mauldin, Doug Kiker, Jack Horner, John Chancellor—the list of journalists as guests at the LBJ ranch seems almost endless. One particular White House correspondent for the *Washington Star* and his wife spent so much time at the ranch they must have wasted hundreds of dollars on hotel rooms in Austin and San Antonio. And this fellow got lots of exclusives for the *Washington Star,* especially on the frequent occasions when Johnson was angry at the *Washington Post.* Most of us felt that his copy often bordered on the sycophantic. Indeed any reporter who played the game by Johnson's rules often faced the choice between access and objectivity. So in my mind any close friendship between president and reporter is suspect.

I read that some such friendships are genuine and durable. That may have been the case with Kennedy and Ben Bradlee. And I can't forget the example of Bill Costello of Mutual Radio. He was one of LBJ's favorites. After heart surgery ended Bill's broadcasting career, Johnson made him an ambassador. But too often these supposed friendships do not survive adversity, meaning sudden attacks of journalistic objectivity. And they often expire when there is an end to presidential need. Take the case of John Chancellor. Because of the importance of NBC, Chancellor was wooed assiduously by LBJ. John's an easy man to get along with and assumed that a real friendship might be blossoming between him and the President. Then Edward R. Murrow who was running Voice of America, died of cancer. Johnson stepped up his courtship of Chancellor. John and his wife were invited to spend the weekend at Camp David. Lyndon and Lady Bird welcomed them as dear family friends. Mingling flattery with calls to patriotic duty, the President insisted that Chancellor become director of the Voice of America. Overwhelmed by the Johnson treatment, Chancellor agreed. But once he was corralled, he never was asked to meet again with his dear friend Lyndon.

Although the Kennedy-Bradlee friendship endured, even that relationship was threatened periodically. In his memoir Bradlee wrote, "Kennedys, by definition, want 110% in their friends, especially those friends in the press, and feel cheated by anything less." *Look* magazine accurately quoted Bradlee in 1961 as saying, "It's almost impossible to write a story they like. Even if a story is quite favorable to their side, they'll find one paragraph to quibble with." Well, the President read Bradlee's statement in *Look* and became more than a little angry. Wrote Bradlee, "That did it. From regular contact, dinner at the White House once and sometimes twice a week, and telephone calls as needed in either direction, to no contact." Kennedy ignored Bradlee for three months. After the two men resumed their friendship Kennedy explained his anger: "Jesus, there you are really plugged in, better than any other reporter except Charley Bartlett, getting one exclusive after another out of this place and what do you do but dump all over us?"

Any reporter thus chastened might well balance his conscience against his zeal for exclusives. In too many instances conscience might lose out to the very human desire to avoid the presidential doghouse and to keep the exclusives coming. But you don't have to be a presidential intimate to feel the lash of presidential anger. No reporter who is doing his job can totally avoid the doghouse or the woodshed. It can happen in the most innocent and innocuous of circumstances. In September 1963, Sandy Vanocur and I were having dinner out at Grand Teton National Park with Pierre Salinger and Kenny O'Donnell. Salinger suddenly turned on me and said, "Cormier, you're nothing but a peeping tom reporter." I couldn't imagine what had prompted this outburst. Well, it turned out he was talking about an insignificant four paragraph story I had written a few weeks earlier about a Kennedy caper at Newport, Rhode Island. The first paragraph couldn't have been more innocent: "President Kennedy and wife Jacqueline starred today in their own home movie." I then reported that a Navy movie cameraman had filmed the Kennedys and friends disembarking from the presidential yacht. Still pretty innocuous. But then I'd gone on to write that Kennedy had suddenly clutched his chest and fallen to the docks spewing red liquid from his mouth. And there were a few more gory details about what obviously was a Kennedy pre-enactment of his own assassination. I just wrote what I saw through binoculars from the boat that Merriman Smith and I had hired, and always did hire, to follow the Kennedys. Only years later did I learn that the Kennedys had been amusing themselves by filming their own version of a James Bond movie.

That story was in terrible taste, Salinger told me. If it was in bad taste for me to write it, I felt it was in bad taste for the President to do it.

In jumping on me, Salinger was simply echoing presidential anger. Kennedy made his own feelings evident by never again addressing me by name. In fact, he ignored me entirely except at news conferences. And on one other occasion, five days before he was killed, he accused me quite wrongly for spying on his after dark activities in New York City.

I can say truthfully that none of this really bothered me. I ignored it. My reporting was in no way dependent on direct access to Kennedy. But what would have happened had he lived and kept me in limbo indefinitely . . . ? I just don't have the answer but I suspect at some point, had his animosity continued, it would have hurt. There also is the ever present possibility that presidential aides, taking a cue from their boss, will stop talking to a reporter who is persona non grata in the Oval Office.

The potential difficulties facing a White House reporter are probably more numerous than our readers and listeners might imagine. The case of Richard Lerner, a former UPI reporter, comes to mind. Lerner had a rather heated argument with Richard Nixon's friend, Bob Abplanalp. Nixon was in no way involved, even indirectly. Nevertheless, the President heard about the argument and instructed Bob Haldeman to bar Lerner from all future flights on Air Force One. This would have been a direct blow to UPI's coverage inasmuch as the competing AP would have continued to have a seat on the presidential plane. Fortunately the White House staff, presumably accustomed to Nixon's sometimes extravagant and intemperate orders, ignored his instruction in this case. What it boils down to is this: If you're friendly with a source, you face pressures to remain friendly and to give 110% to the cause. If you're neutral or hostile, you risk retaliation and a possible loss of sources.

And there is a third more direct threat to a reporter's livelihood. Angry presidents sometimes try to get reporters fired. The prize example is Kennedy's effort to have Dave Halberstam removed as *New York Times* reporter in Vietnam. And we're familiar with Nixon's attempt to get Dan Rather off the White House beat, both of which failed. But failure is not inevitable. Lyndon Johnson proved that it can be done. The victim in Johnson's case was a White House correspondent for one of the three major networks. In terms that were mild for LBJ, the President accused the broadcaster of being impertinent during a conversation on Air Force One. I happened to agree with Johnson, although I didn't say so. And I assumed that his mild rebuke would end it. But I.was wrong. Acting quietly and with great subtlty, Johnson retaliated. Through aides he leaked two major exclusives to the offending reporter. They were so important they led the evening news broadcasts. There was only one problem. The leaks were totally false. The broadcaster was removed from the White House and soon left the business.

Any gift horse provided by Lyndon Johnson had to be looked at squarely in the mouth. A few days before Christmas 1964, the White House limousine delivered to my home a giftwrapped package from the President. The box was empty. And I'll never know if Johnson tried to get me fired a few months later but it sure seemed like it at the time. Ironically, the incident stemmed from one of his recurrent efforts to woo White House reporters. After walking around the South Lawn with about six of us, he took us into the Oval Office. Once again he said, "I'm going to help you all become big men in your profession." He promised each of us a luncheon in his private dining room and he added specific instructions: "You write to the six or seven people in your organization who can do you the most good and you say, 'Dear Joe, I'm invited to have lunch with the President of the United States in the family quarters of the White House on such and such a date at such and such a time and I would be pleased if you could join us.'" I managed to get the first luncheon appointment on May 12, 1965. But I did not wheel and deal as LBJ had suggested. The guest list for AP was prepared by my bosses.

On the appointed day we met in the upstairs dining room with the President, George Reedy, Jack Valenti, McGeorge Bundy, Bill Moyers, Horace Busby, and Doug Cater. Johnson told our general manager, then Wes Gallager, to sit at his right hand and for me to sit next to Gallager. Rubbing his eyes and looking forlorn, Johnson began by saying, "I'm awfully tired today. I was up until four thirty in the morning reading Jack Bell's book." Well, Jack had just written a book called *The Johnson Treatment* and naturally Gallager lept in and said, "How did you like it, Mr. President?" Putting on a long face Johnson replied, "I found it rather entertaining but unfortunately it doesn't have any first hand information. When I was up on the Hill I used to see old Jack all the time. But since I've been President I just don't get to see old Jack anymore. So, as a consequence, in order to write that book poor old Jack had to rely on erroneous clips of things that Frank had written that he, in turn, had gotten second hand from somebody else." Well, I thought that was a hell of a way to make me a big man in my profession! And I don't think it was any accident.

Johnson probably was the biggest schemer ever to be President. He hardly did anything without calculation. I'm convinced he plotted the whole scenario in advance. What I don't know is his motive.

But Johnson wasn't through with me yet. Later in our luncheon meeting he leaned across the table and told me, "You caught me by surprise with your first question at the last press conference. You tried to get me to make a damn fool of myself." Two weeks earlier this was the question that I'd asked Johnson at a televised news conference. "Mr. President, do you think any of the participants in the national discussion on Vietnam could appropriately be likened to the appeasers of twenty-five or thirty years ago?" And Johnson replied, "I don't believe in characterizing people with labels. I think you do a great disservice when you engage in name-calling. We want honest, forthright discussion in this country." Well, at the luncheon table Johnson stared at me and clasped his hands as if in prayer and he said, "Every night when I go to bed I kneel down and I thank the dear God that he didn't let Frank Cormier make a fool out of me." I had asked the question because Johnson, off the record, had been engaging in unrestrained labelling and name-calling. To him, Senator J. William Fullbright was another Neville Chamberlain. I simply had tried to get Johnson to say publicly what he'd been saying privately.

Despite our acrimonious luncheon Lyndon Johnson and I coexisted, sometimes quite amicably, for another four years. Which brings me to another point. Presidents need reporters just as much as reporters need presidents. On the recurrent occasions when the White House press corps is at odds with presidents and their assistants, we console ourselves by saying we were here before they came and we'll be here after they've gone. It's a thought that tends to bolster our sense of independence.

In conclusion, I must resort to a truism, if not a cliché. Reporters must not only establish their independence, but preserve it. Maintaining a more than casual friendship with a president clearly places independence in jeopardy. And if independence means unpleasant trips to the presidential woodshed, so be it. Our editors must insist on our independence and our readers and listeners should welcome it. Thank you.

MS. THOMAS: That was absolutely fantastic.

MR. CORMIER: Oh, you've heard all those stories.

MS. THOMAS: You know, Frank said that Nixon didn't get Rather. That's true, but eventually don't you think that the network kind of bowed, basically? But not at the time.

MR. CORMIER: Yes, but Nixon was out of the White House, Ford was in. So it could be—

MS. THOMAS: But everybody attributes it to that, the challenging of Nixon by Rather.

MR. DEAKIN: CBS waited long enough so they couldn't actually pin it on them. But Nixon was certainly the reason.

Question: How far does it go? I have a friend in the university world who is a critic, maybe the earliest critic, and he always maintained that he was audited on his income tax. Does it get that far with reporters?

MR. CORMIER: I never was audited, ever. I don't know. I would question whether any other president tried to intercede with the IRS.

MR. DEAKIN: Nixon, for instance, in one month put in 60 to 80 requests for government retaliation against journalists whose coverage he considered unfair. This comes from Jeb Magruder's memo to Bob Haldeman on Oct. 17, 1969.

MS. THOMAS: Kennedy sent the FBI around on this.

MR. CORMIER: He was checking up on what Bethlehem Steel people had said at their annual meeting, I think, to reporters.

MR. DEAKIN: This is one reason why Watergate came out—not the only reason, but it's one of them. Because what happened when Nixon tried to get the FBI and the CIA and the IRS to retaliate against his enemies was that they started leaking like a sieve, in self-defense. I'm convinced these were some of the places where Woodward and Bernstein were getting their information.

MR. BLACKFORD: The IRS?

MR. DEAKIN: The IRS and other bureaucrats whose independence was being threatened by Nixon. Once people got the idea that their income tax could be audited for saying something, for free speech, the credibility of the IRS would be down the drain. I know they started leaking—I can't document that they started leaking to Woodward and Bernstein—but I know they started leaking. I know other reporters they did leak to. They were fighting back against Nixon.

I'll tell you something that happened to me. I will just tell you the story and you can make your own interpretation. I haven't come to any conclusion. It was in August of 1973. We were out at San Clemente, and it was the height of the Ervin investigation. John Dean was singing like a canary. And Nixon held a press conference. Remember that, the August '73 press conference on the lawn at San Clemente? A very sunny day.

MR. CORMIER: That's where he named Kissinger Secretary of State, isn't it?

MR. DEAKIN: Yes, that's right. He started out by announcing Bill Rogers's resignation and the appointment of Kissinger. Then the press conference proceeded. Most of the questions were about Watergate. After about twenty minutes to half an hour of questions about Watergate, Nixon broke in and said: Now, wait a minute. We've had twenty minutes of questions about Watergate, and nothing about all the other important matters affecting the United States, all the other things the American people are interested in. He was setting us up as the villains. We were the bad guys. We were fixated on Watergate and weren't giving the American people the president's views on all these other important issues. So he read us this little lecture and then he turned to me. I'm convinced that he knew full well that I would ask another Watergate question. So I asked him a question about the Huston report, which was a report approved by the president and left in effect for five days. They always said they had canceled it after five days, but Ziegler would never show us a piece of paper canceling it. Month after month we said, "Where's the cancelation? Show us the order canceling it." The order never was shown to us.

MS. THOMAS: This was the report on domestic spying, I take it.

MR. DEAKIN: This was the report in which the President of the United States approved illegal acts, breakings and enterings, the whole business. Illegal actions. And it was in effect for at least five days. So I'd become convinced, after the Huston plan came to light, that either Nixon would be impeached or forced out of office, or we'd have anarchy because the president is sworn to uphold the law. The Constitution specifies an oath to execute the law. So when Nixon recognized me, I said that I had studied the Huston plan. I recounted what it provided—domestic wiretapping, surveillance, breaking and entering, all kinds of illegal stuff. And then I said: "Mr. President, if you were in Congress, wouldn't you be considering impeachment proceedings against an elected official who had violated his oath of office?" That was the first time impeachment had been mentioned on national television. Nixon didn't like it, but that was the end of it for the moment. I got back to the Surf and Sand. I had just finished my story and some White House functionary came and said, "Ziegler wants to see you." Ziegler had an office at the Surf and Sand—the press hotel. So I went up to his office and I said, hello, and he said, hello, and I sat down. And he said: "Why do you ask questions like that? You have a lovely wife and a wonderful child."

MS. THOMAS: If someone in the Mafia had said that, I would have said that—

MR. DEAKIN: He could have meant, why are you such a curmudgeon when you have such a nice wife and child? Why are you such a son-of-a-bitch when you have such a nice wife and boy? Or he could have meant something else. Feelings were running high. I don't know.

Question: Sandy's talked in other connections about this, but what about trying to establish things about your personal lives. Does it go that far? Doing the Martin Luther King thing, putting agents on you—

MR. DEAKIN: During the Nixon administration, they wiretapped reporters as well as members of the National Security staff.

MS. THOMAS: Henry Brandon.

MR. DEAKIN: They wiretapped Brandon. Of course they thought Brandon was an agent of British intelligence and, of all things, Czech intelligence.

MR. CORMIER: And no one ever found out what those electricians were doing in Dan Rather's house.

MR. DEAKIN: Of course, we had the electricians at our house, too. That was another thing. While I was out in California the electricians were out in front of our house and Doris, my wife, wondered what the hell was going on. They subpoenaed our long-distance records without telling us. I found out later they were trying to track down how we got the Pentagon Papers. They wiretapped Brandon, they wiretapped someone from the *New York Times*. Who did they wiretap on the *New York Times* that they thought Halperin (Morton Halperin, then of the NSC staff) was talking to?

MR. CORMIER: Was it Gelb?

MR. DEAKIN: Yes, I think it was Les Gelb. They wiretapped Gelb and they wiretapped Brandon and several other reporters. They did a lot of things. They had an enemies list. They were out for blood.

MR. CORMIER: I thought perhaps you were referring to the sexual pecadillos or something by members of the press corps. Lyndon Johnson had an insatiable appetite for gossip. And while he was President, the guys were facilitating our problems with the Secret Service and security. They started assigning a Secret Service agent, sometimes two, to go with us on all trips. He usually would make the after hours rounds with you, and what not. Whether he was reporting or not I don't know, but I do know—and it's no secret at all—that Johnson would call up people in Austin, if that's where we were, late at night, he often called Joe Laitin who will tell you all about it. Johnson would want to know who went out with whom and who was this, that and the next thing. Joe sometimes would just make up outrageous things.

MR. DEAKIN: Now, you talk about seduction. I'll tell you a seduction story. During the Kennedy administration—and Kennedy was very seductive, as Ben Bradlee points out—they held a state dinner at Mt. Vernon for Mohammad Ayub Khan, the president of Pakistan. Doris and I were invited, not as reporters but as guests. And it was just an absolutely beautiful evening. I'm not going to go into lengthy detail, but it was the best party I've ever been to in my life. They had a little reception line at Mt. Vernon. First there was Kennedy, then Ayub Khan, and then there was Jackie, and then Ayub Khan's daughter. Kennedy greeted me as I came through the reception line, and we exchanged a few words. Then he passed me on to Ayub Khan, who was British-educated, and about six feet four tall, a very formidable man. He gave me what I call a Sandhurst stare. Ayub Khan didn't even say hello. It was obvious that in Pakistan journalists were things that crawled out from under rocks. He snubbed me completely. He was obviously wondering what a scribbler was doing at a state dinner for the great Khan. Kennedy saw all this. I was about to pass on to Jackie when Kennedy grabs my arm and pulls me back and plunks me right down in front of Khan again. And he says to Khan: "Mr. Deakin is a distinguished journalist for one of our most distinguished newspapers." Now, how in hell was I supposed to resist that? That's seduction!

MR. THOMPSON: What is the pay-off? Are there any stories of great national importance that one of you could not have written if you had not had as much access as you may have had to a public figure?

MR. CORMIER: Oh, I'm sure there are.

MR. DEAKIN: And it also works in reverse, because there are stories reporters suppress. Bill Lawrence, in his memoirs, tells about four or five that he suppressed, including the fact that Dean Rusk was going to be named secretary of state. (Lawrence was a veteran reporter for the *New York Times* and later for ABC).

MS. THOMAS: But they get a lot. He got Kennedy's financial disclosures, and so forth. I mean, Kennedy's financial disclosures and so forth.

MR. DEAKIN: What stories have reporters got as a result of this access to the president? Well, I'll tell you about John Pomfret of the *New York Times*. Pomfret had stood up to Johnson at one point by refusing to ask a planted question at a press conference. Anytime you stood up to Johnson you found that the other side of a bully was a coward. So Johnson called in Pomfret and gave him three or four exclusive stories to coddle him, to seduce him.

MS. THOMAS: You know, I think in terms of seduction, I was amused at the quirks of fate because Teddy White had always considered himself so close to presidents, especially to Nixon and he was getting one exclusive after another. Well, after the Watergate debacle, White wrote a book entitled, *How Can You Do This To Me?* How on earth can you do this, not to the country, not to the democracy, but me!

73

It was an incredible kind of ego trip. Nixon went out of his way to introduce him in China. Really ingratiated.

MR. BLACKFORD: Did Nixon make much effort to curry the favor of the press?

MR. CORMIER: Well, occasionally. He had in '69, before his first overseas trip, after he'd been in office a month, a nice pre-departure cocktail party for us.

MS. THOMAS: Care and feeding of the press through that whole campaign. Don't answer any questions but take care of food and good hotels. Make sure they get good meals. Make sure that all their needs are taken care of, but don't tell them anything.

MR. CORMIER: He also had a couple of Christmas parties.

MR. JONES: Frank, I wonder if you'd talk just a bit about seniority in the White House press corps. Are there some consequences of being there a long time?

MR. CORMIER: I suppose there are, but I don't think they're overriding, by any means. One consequence of having been there before is things do have a way of recurring and maybe then you are able to put some things in a broader context. That's the most valuable thing.

MS. THOMAS: Every president is new, in a sense. You start all over, yourself, in a way. He puts his own stamp on things. A lot of the networks—not this time around—but the networks will often change their key people. Oftentimes a newspaper will change.

MR. DEAKIN: Newspapers have started doing that now. I think it stems from the network example, don't you?

MS. THOMAS: A former colleague now covers Reagan. He was with UPI many years. He was our Sacramento Bureau Chief. Then he went with the *L.A. Times,* became their political person. Now he's assigned to the White House because of having intimately covered Reagan for many years. I think the one we know about in AP was Tony Vaccaro who covered the Senate, covered Truman, and they were friends, weren't they?

MR. CORMIER: Sure, they played poker together. On his second day in office Truman was being driven to work and saw him on the street and said "Come in, Tony." So Tony went down to the White House with Truman. The AP, at that point, I'm sure had made no decision to assign Tony Vaccaro to the White House. But when they heard Harry had hauled him down there, he was there for the rest of Harry's tenure.

MR. JONES: Are there other examples of that?

MR. DEAKIN: Did you mention Sandy Vanocur? He was out in

Chicago but because he knew Kennedy, they brought him in and assigned him to the White House when Kennedy became president.

MS. THOMAS: Oftentimes a reporter was assigned to cover a campaign, sort of just automatically. Donaldson did not cover the White House but he was assigned to cover Carter—it started in the '76 campaign, from January on. And by the time the election rolled around, he was really on the camera.

MR. DEAKIN: Judy Woodruff covered Carter during the campaign from Atlanta and when Carter got elected, Judy was assigned to the White House. This has now become pretty standard.

MR. JONES: Any examples of where the president actively seeks to exert pressure to bring on a certain person, not just having developed a rapport?

MS. THOMAS: I think that's happened a little bit.

MR. DEAKIN: For example, trying to get someone kicked off a story, the classic one being Kennedy with Halberstam during Vietnam.

MS. THOMAS: Well, if you have a Texas president you're going to have more Texas reporters. If you have a California president, you're going to have more California reporters.

MR. THOMPSON: What about you, Smitty and Helen, in terms of special favors because of seniority and because of the first question business?

MS. THOMAS: Well, you know by tradition the wire service—it's not in concrete, it's a great privilege because you don't have to—in the past you didn't have to stand up and scream like a banshee for attention. And believe me, we love this privilege but it is strictly tradition, it could be changed at any time that you rotate. So far we've been able to keep it in place even though I'm sure the networks are probably getting very unhappy with it. There aren't very many other traditions except the "Thank you, Mr. President."

We used to be the only ones manning the barricades. Now the networks are there morning to night, really long hours like from five-thirty, six o'clock for the morning broadcast. If there is anything going on where the White House will have a role, or they're going to get Ed Meese out on the lawn, even at that hour, they do stay a long time. But, they are performing a role that the wire services always have.

MR. THOMPSON: One thing we haven't gotten into in any of these discussions, except historically, is the process wherein people sat around press rooms in the morning and went to the nearby theatres in the afternoon because there was so little to do. Could you tell us just a little about your hours today with the Reagan administration?

MS. THOMAS: Well, I try to get there about seven-thirty or

quarter to eight mainly for my own edification. Because you should read the papers, you at least glance through the *Post* and the *New York Times* to start your day. You also should call up the story if it was an Iranian crisis every day, you know, what's happened in Iran, the Falklands, things that are really happening so you have some preparation. By nine-fifteen Larry Speakes has initiated his morning briefing where you get a rundown on the president's day. You also find out what subject they've chosen for you to cover *per se,* or whether you'll get to cover at all. Many days will go by, as I say, where we don't see him and even though it seems to be a legitimate thing to cover they don't let us.

We have that briefing, then we go and file, say, reaction to the unemployment figures. Then at noon we have a full-scale briefing where everybody comes in from all over town. And through the day we cover the things that you can and every day is different. If there is a head of state, we could work on until midnight covering the social part and so forth.

MR. JONES: Do you sit down with Speakes before the press conference and talk about timing or any kind of arrangements?

MS. THOMAS: No. We always know if it's televised; unless they tell you otherwise, it's a half hour. What you do try to find out is if the president's going to make an opening statement. And if he does, if it takes any of our time, we get it back on the other end.

MR. DEAKIN: Are they trying to plant any questions?

MS. THOMAS: If they are I don't know about it. They can pretty well tell what we're going to ask from front row, in terms that they know we want hard news. They don't know what's coming out of left field. And all the women are wearing red dresses to get Reagan's eye!

MR. CORMIER: Have you ever felt the need to know in advance you were going to let the news conference go over the half hour and talk to the networks about it?

MS. THOMAS: We haven't done it so far and nobody's put any pressure on us to do it.

MR. CORMIER: Back when Nixon was going long stretches without them, I was always trying to make them a little longer. I didn't have to but I always checked with the networks to make sure it wasn't going to cost them a hundred million dollars or something, and I never, except on one occasion, had a network say other than let it go as long as you want. One of the networks one night had a hell of a conflict, I forget what it was.

MS. THOMAS: You get an evil eye from either Speakes or Gergin come the witching hour so you begin to—. A couple of times Reagan really plays the part of Mr. Nice Guy. If a hand is raised, he really doesn't want to turn away and that's very nice.

MR. CORMIER: Well, both Nixon and Carter said "Thank you" on different occasions when they thought it had gone too long.

MR. DEAKIN: One time after you had said thank you I asked if he would give us some more time.

MS. THOMAS: Great tension.

MR. DEAKIN: There had been a three-month gap between press conferences. You said, "Thank you," and I said, "You haven't had a press conference in three months and we have a few more questions."

MR. CORMIER: Did he answer you?

MR. DEAKIN: Yes, he gave us some more time.

MR. BLACKFORD: Who was this, Nixon or—?

MR. DEAKIN: Nixon.

MS. THOMAS: One day I got up at a Reagan news conference, and he does have long answers. So you really look kind of silly— you're half-way out of your seat trying to catch it right in between. So, I was half-way out of the seat and Mary McGrory jumped up—and I had said "Thank you, Mr. President," so Reagan looked at her. She asked about the tithing and I said under my breath, "I told you so," and he heard it, bad as his hearing is. He said, "From now on I'll listen to Helen."

BLACKFORD: Getting to work at seven-thirty, what time is an average day, what time do you wrap it up?

MS. THOMAS: Again you don't know. Sometimes you go home at seven, sometimes six-thirty, sometimes eight o'clock. It just depends on when the story is done or when you feel you can leave it. We write the pm's, we write the am's, and we write the overnights, and it could go on. When you leave at six o'clock, even on Friday, as I say, those are kind of death days, you don't really know. Sometimes they'll say the lid is on and you don't quite trust them because things are happening in the world. I think the TV correspondents really at the White House are terrific. They have good sources, they can call up someone, people want to talk to TV people. Oftentimes they'll have something on the six-thirty news that you will get a call back on and you say "Gee, I've been there all day, is that really what happened?"

MR. THOMPSON: Helen, can you ever ask a complex question at a press conference? Example: Wouldn't it be valuable to know why the Argentinians miscalculated in believing that we would be on their side in the Falkland Islands?

MS. THOMAS: You think they miscalculated?

MR. DEAKIN: It was the U.S. that changed. They had every reason to believe that we were going to be at least neutral.

MS. THOMAS: You think that's why they went in?

MR. THOMPSON: Reston and others are beginning to say that now. But can you ever ask that kind of a question at a press conference?

MS. THOMAS: Of course. Of course you can.

MR. CORMIER: You won't get an answer, but you can ask it.

MR. DEAKIN: Some reporters have been known, including yours truly, for asking long and involved questions.

MS. THOMAS: You would put it that way. I would say: Why did you mislead the Argentinians into thinking that? He would answer your question, but would not answer mine because they see some sort of a trick in it.

I think that Reagan would try to answer but you wouldn't quite know what he was saying. I found the MX basing decision, when they decided—and they've changed their minds since that a few times—they would put the MX missile in the Minuteman silos. Well, Reagan made the announcement, and we started asking him, and he said, "You answer the questions." He turned to Weinberger. On anything in foreign policy he turns to Haig, "He'll answer the questions."

MR. DEAKIN: Sometimes you can't understand what the president is saying. You get this with some presidents. My favorite was Eisenhower. It was almost impossible sometimes to understand what Eisenhower was saying when he answered a question—And my favorite was the answer—I don't remember the question, but the answer was: "I have held for a long time several things about that."

MR. THOMPSON: The Casey Stengel of politics.

MS. THOMAS: That's true.

MR. BLACKFORD: Some people are saying that sometimes he deliberately did that and meant just the opposite?

MR. DEAKIN: We should talk about that. It is the revisionist idea. That's the theory of Professor Greenstein at Princeton. I disagree. Greenstein says that Ike was doing this as part of his "hidden-hand" presidency. The mangled syntax was intentional, to conceal his intentions. Greenstein cites instances when Eisenhower was correcting something that Dulles had said, and so forth. I was at those press conferences, and I do not a agree with Professor Greenstein. In one case Eisenhower was just misinformed, he didn't know, and in the other case all he was trying to do was clean up a mistake that had been made. He was smart enough to do that. But this hidden hand stuff—I don't agree.

MS. THOMAS: And I think that one of the most articulate presidents—of course Kennedy was very articulate and had the warmth and wit—was Carter, I mean—complete sentences, one word followed another, logical thought for whatever his point of view was. He was a man who did express himself well.

MR. DEAKIN: Yes, Carter was easy to follow.

MR. THOMPSON: I'm interested in your reaction to one of Jody Powell's comments. When we asked why they didn't continue with more press conferences, he said, "Because we found unless we had something important to announce they weren't worthwhile. They were counter-productive."

MS. THOMAS: Well, from their point of view anything is.

MR. DEAKIN: Unfortunately, they leave the American people out.

MS. THOMAS: This is often a reason why a press secretary will say we're not going to have a news briefing today, we have nothing to announce. We say, well, we have a lot of questions and that certainly goes for a president. We don't want him to make announcements and use our time. He can announce anything any time.

MR. CORMIER: Powell was not the first to say presidents shouldn't have press conferences except when "we have something to say."

MS. THOMAS: That's right. They all want to do that, it's part of the news management. And they certainly don't want to have a news conference when things are going wrong, or when it's a touchy atmosphere. It has nothing to do with national security or anything else. It's embarrassing.

MR. CORMIER: It has something to do with the Gallup polls, certainly.

MS. THOMAS: They live by that.

MR. BLACKFORD: How frequently did Kennedy have press conferences?

MR. CORMIER: Roughly every two weeks except during hiatuses, and he had one hiatus of about three months, as I remember.

MR. DEAKIN: Kennedy held 64 press conferences in three years, which is an average of .4 press conferences a week or almost two a month.

MR. BLACKFORD: How many has Reagan had so far?

MR. DEAKIN: Nine formal ones. It's been going steadily down, if you want the figures. Roosevelt held 998 press conferences in twelve years. It is not quite true that he held them twice a week. He held them twice a week in peace time. When the war came he cut them down to once a week on some weeks, but the total still came out to more than six a month. Truman held 322 press conferences in seven years, which was almost four a month. Eisenhower held 193 in eight years, which was two a month. Kennedy held sixty-four in three years, which was almost two a month. Johnson held 135 in five years, which was two a month. Nixon held thirty-nine in five and a half year, which was .5 a month. That is, one-half press conference a month. Carter had held fifty-nine up to September of 1980—I'm sorry I don't have it after that—which was 1.3 a month. The trend has been steadily down.

MR. THOMPSON: I'm sorry we must break it off with that; we've run out of time. I wish to thank all of you for participating, particularly Helen, Frank, and Jim. It's been a fascinating session and will be a significant contribution to the study of the presidency and the press. Thank you.

VIRGINIA PARTICIPANTS

Staige Blackford	Editor, *Virginia Quarterly Review*
Charles O. Jones	Gooch Professor of Government
James Latimer	Columnist and reporter, *Richmond Times Dispatch*
Kenneth W. Thompson	Director, Miller Center of Public Affairs
James S. Young	Director, Presidency Research Project of the Miller Center